Our Nation's Capital
Pro Bono Publico Ideas proffered by ARTHUR COTTON MOORE FAIA

Our Nation's Capital
Pro Bono Publico Ideas
proffered by ARTHUR COTTON MOORE FAIA

IA&A INTERNATIONAL ARTS AND ARTISTS

Copyright© 2017 by Arthur Cotton Moore
ISBN: 978-0-692-81344-7
Library of Congress Control Number: 2016920179

All rights reserved, including the right to reproduce this book or portions thereof in any form whatsoever—each form shall enjoy these same copyright protections. A digital version of this book will simultaneously be published.

No part of this book (in any of its forms) may be used, reproduced or distributed in any medium or by any means, or stored in a database or retrieval system, without the prior written permission of the author.

This book comprises ideas for building projects that were solely imagined, created, and graphically rendered by the author, each of which enjoys these same copyright protections. It is hoped that some portion of these projects will be brought to reality by others, whom the author could accommodate by granting copyright permissions through written licenses.

author contact:
info@arthurcottonmoore.com
www.arthurcottonmoore.com

Published in the United States of America
by International Arts & Artists
9 Hillyer Court NW
Washington, DC 20008
www.artsandartists.org

Designer: Deanna Luu, IA&A Design Studio
Copy Editors: David Walker and Seth Dorcus

Printed through Four Colour Print Group
2410 Frankfort Avenue
Louisville, Kentucky 40206
Printed in China

International Arts & Artists is a nonprofit arts service organization dedicated to promoting cross-cultural understanding and exposure to the arts internationally.

IA&A | INTERNATIONAL ARTS AND ARTISTS

Also by Arthur Cotton Moore

The Powers of Preservation: New Life for Urban Historic Places
Copyright© 1998 by The McGraw-Hill Companies, Inc.
ISBN: 0-07-043394-1

Interruption of the Cocktail Hour: A Washington Yarn of Art, Murder, and the Attempted Assassination of the President
Copyright© 2014 by Arthur Cotton Moore
ISBN 10: 1500776610
ISBN 13: 9781500776619
Library of Congress Control Number: 2014921985
CreateSpace Independent Publishing Platform
North Charleston, South Carolina

Image Credits

Map data courtesy of Google, Google Earth Pro: Cover, Pages 41, 42, 45, 65, 66, 70, 75, 85, and 92

Carol M. Highsmith: Page 31

Every reasonable effort has been made to identify copyright ownership for several images. Corrections will be included in subsequent editions.

For Wolf von Eckardt
1918–1995
The Architecture Critic of The Washington Post
1963–1981

TABLE OF CONTENTS

PAGE 09 INTRODUCTION

CHAPTER 1: GEORGETOWN

page 11	Planning a New Georgetown Waterfront
page 12	The Terraced K Street Plan
page 13	How to Replace the Whitehurst Freeway
page 14	Spiral Ramp from Key Bridge

CHAPTER 2: AIRPORTS: RONALD REAGAN (NATIONAL) + WASHINGTON DULLES INTERNATIONAL

page 15	Replace National Airport with a New Town, and a Fast Rail Line to Dulles
page 16	A Rosslyn Air Terminal for Direct Bus/Mobile Lounge Connection to Airplanes
page 17	The Rosslyn Air Terminal

CHAPTER 3: THE JOHN F. KENNEDY CENTER FOR THE PERFORMING ARTS

page 18	The Kennedy Center Steps + A Loop of Ferryboat Connections
page 19	Structure of Proposed Steps
page 21	Rendering of Proposed Steps
page 22	Promenade Between Georgetown and the Kennedy Center
page 24	Connecting Rosslyn, Georgetown, and the Kennedy Center by Water

CHAPTER 4: ALTERNATIVES TO DEMOLITION

page 25	Saving the Old Post Office Building
page 26	Bridging the Two Faces of Washington
page 27	1973 *Progressive Architecture* Magazine Cover
page 28	A Proposal to Save the Third Church of Christ, Scientist
page 30	Saving the L'Enfant and McMillan Plans through Alternative Site Planning
page 32	A Continuous Maryland Avenue
page 33	Underground Museum Connection
page 34	A Second Alternative Site

CHAPTER 5: THE WHITE HOUSE GROUNDS

page 35	Re-Opening Pennsylvania Avenue with Enhanced White House Security
page 36	Gates on Pennsylvania Avenue to Restrict Truck Traffic
page 37	Current Default Use of Pennsylvania Avenue in Front of the White House

CHAPTER 6: THE WASHINGTON METROPOLITAN AREA

page 38	Development of Maryland Avenue Pursuant to the L'Enfant Plan
page 39	Conception of a Future Maryland Avenue to the Capitol
page 41	Sites to be Developed
page 42	One Hundred Years Later
page 43	Intermodal Commuter Train Station
page 44	The Northeast Corridor High-Speed Train that Never Stops
page 45	Geothermal Energy Saving Strategies
page 46	Solar Panels on the Kennedy Center Roof
page 47	Metro Car Housing for our Homeless Population
page 50	Suggestions for the New Convention Center
page 51	A New Way for Downtown Urban Renewal
page 52	Pop-Up Retail at the Tysons Corner Silver Line

CHAPTER 7: INVITATIONS TO CREATE CONCEPT DESIGNS

page 53	A Roof for the Carter Barron Amphitheatre
page 55	Anacostia Performing Arts Center
page 57	A Patent Museum at the Commerce Department
page 58	Fort Lincoln: A New Town in Town
page 59	New Uses for St. Elizabeths West Campus

CHAPTER 8: FEDERAL GOVERNMENT BUILDINGS

page 61	The FBI Building's Blank Wall on Pennsylvania Avenue (1998)
page 62	Keeping the FBI in Washington on Fallow Federal Land (2013)
page 63	The John Adams Memorial in the John Adams Building. The Library of Congress

CHAPTER 9: THE NATIONAL MALL AND THE MONUMENTAL CORE

page 64	Happy 100th Birthday of the National Park Service
page 65	Amenity for Visitors to the Washington Monument Grounds
page 66	Alternative Sites for Festivals Removed from the Mall
page 67	Linking the Mall Via Memorial Bridges
page 70	17th Street Levee, Linking the Washington Monument Grounds to the Lincoln Memorial Area
page 73	Enhancing the Scope of the District of Columbia War Memorial
page 74	L'Enfant Festival Promenade: Linking the Mall to the Southwest Waterfront

CHAPTER 10: AN ARCHITECTURAL MODEL OF OUR NATION'S CAPITAL

page 79	A Pavilion on the Vacant Land Adjacent to the National Building Museum
page 79	Ground Floor Facilities
page 81	Upper Level of Model
page 81	Lower Level of Model
page 82	Remote Control Camera-Cars Around Dupont Circle
page 83	Aerial View of the Pavilion

CHAPTER 11: THE NATIONAL MALL UNDERGROUND

page 85	Access to and Exits from the Underground Garage
page 85	General Services Administration Photograph of the 2006 Flood
page 86	Our Viable Response to Flooding in this Location
page 87	Flood Control, Irrigation, and a Geothermal Field
page 88	Tour Bus/Museum Visitor Parking
page 88	Holding Reservoir for Constitution Avenue Flood Waters
page 89	Lower Level Geothermal Field of Wells
page 90	Washington Harbour Flooding Prototype
page 92	Method of Detoxifying Flood Waters from Constitution Avenue
page 93	Visitor Center/Irrigation Cistern
page 94	Entrance Pavilions
page 95	A Mechanical/Robotic Parking System for Museum Visitors' Cars
page 96	How the Robotic Garage Works
page 97	Inside the Robotic Garage
page 98	Tour Bus Entrance to the Robotic Garage
page 99	Retention of Storm Flood Waters from Constitution Avenue
page 99	Car Entrance from 12th Street Ramp
page 100	The Visitor Center Main Hall
page 101	Barrel-Vaulted Main Hall in the Visitor Center

CHAPTER 12: OUR MASTER PLAN OF THE NATIONAL MALL EXPANDED FOR THE 21st CENTURY

page 103	Existing Configuration
page 105	Benefits of Expanding the Mall
page 106	Section Through Site Plan for the Supreme Court

PAGE 109   OUR WORLD CAPITAL IN THE 21st CENTURY

PAGE 111   ABOUT THE AUTHOR

INTRODUCTION

After fulfilling the required three-year apprenticeship working under the supervision of a licensed architect (Chloethiel Woodard Smith FAIA, in my case), I was qualified to take the Washington, D.C. license exam—five days of written and design tests and one oral exam. I passed on the first try—a good omen; my dream of becoming an Architect had come true.

In 1965, with a copy of my passport to the world of Architecture in my pocket, I quit my job, got on my bike, and rode around the Federal City for hours and hours, during which I decided—being unemployed, without paying clients or prospects—to make the city my first client. (Decades later, even when working on clients' projects, in the back of my mind, I was still working for their client: the public.)

As a sixth-generation Washingtonian, and a relative of Senator James McMillan (1901–1902 McMillan Plan), I've always felt an allegiance to, and patriotic pride in, our Nation's Capital. To this day, I treasure my bond with the city and its history, and my promise to myself to be in the conversation about its future all the days of my life.

I've used up several bikes on my regular weekend rides since then, going all over the city looking for opportunities in the public arena where I could make a positive contribution.

Early on, I realized that the only way to maintain the integrity of this vocation, and to exercise the agency—the freedom—it deserved, was within a strict *pro bono publico* environment: there could be no clients, no compensation by money or favor, and no pursuit of architectural commissions. I would personally do the work without involving the architects in my firm.

Only after about ten years into this saga, when I learned to balance these two very different practices, did I fully embrace the joy of volunteering a portion of my professional services—it had become one of the most rewarding and satisfying activities of my life. Not only was it the best way for me to give back to my hometown, but it gave me valuable and unimaginably complex challenges available no other way—interweaving politics, testimony, engineering, architecture, landscape architecture, real estate development, lobbying, and master planning into a practical, credible, and feasible tapestry of solutions for a hugely variant collection of would-be projects.

These tapestries achieved their level of reality by my stepping—uninvited and mostly unwelcomed—onto the thickly guarded turf of D.C. and Federal Government agencies, which naturally reacted unenthusiastically at times because they came from the outside. When a former Associate Regional Director of the National Park Service called me a fomenter, I was complimented.

Except for the five requests for conceptual designs, I imagined and created these ideas, and personally drew, rendered, sketched, and generated each image (with computer tech help on two of them).

This body of work is being published in digital and limited print form because—essentially—the only people who know about it are those who kindly and generously allowed me into their purview—into their conversation—for which I am forever grateful.

ACM
Washington, D.C., June 2017

1 GEORGETOWN

This was painted on the wall of the Washington Flour Plant: "The objectionable odors you may notice in this area do not originate from this plant."

The smelly Hopfenmaier Rendering Plant

Lower Georgetown when it was an industrial slum, circa 1960.

PLANNING A NEW GEORGETOWN WATERFRONT
(below M Street)

Drawing of the envisioned new waterfront for the Georgetown Planning Council. The National Capital Planning Commission merely published this drawing in its 1967 Green Book, as its way of dealing with the controversial and politically difficult Georgetown Waterfront.

THE TERRACED K STREET PLAN

TERRACED K STREET

SHARP INCLINE LEVELED OUT TO MEET TERRACED K STREET

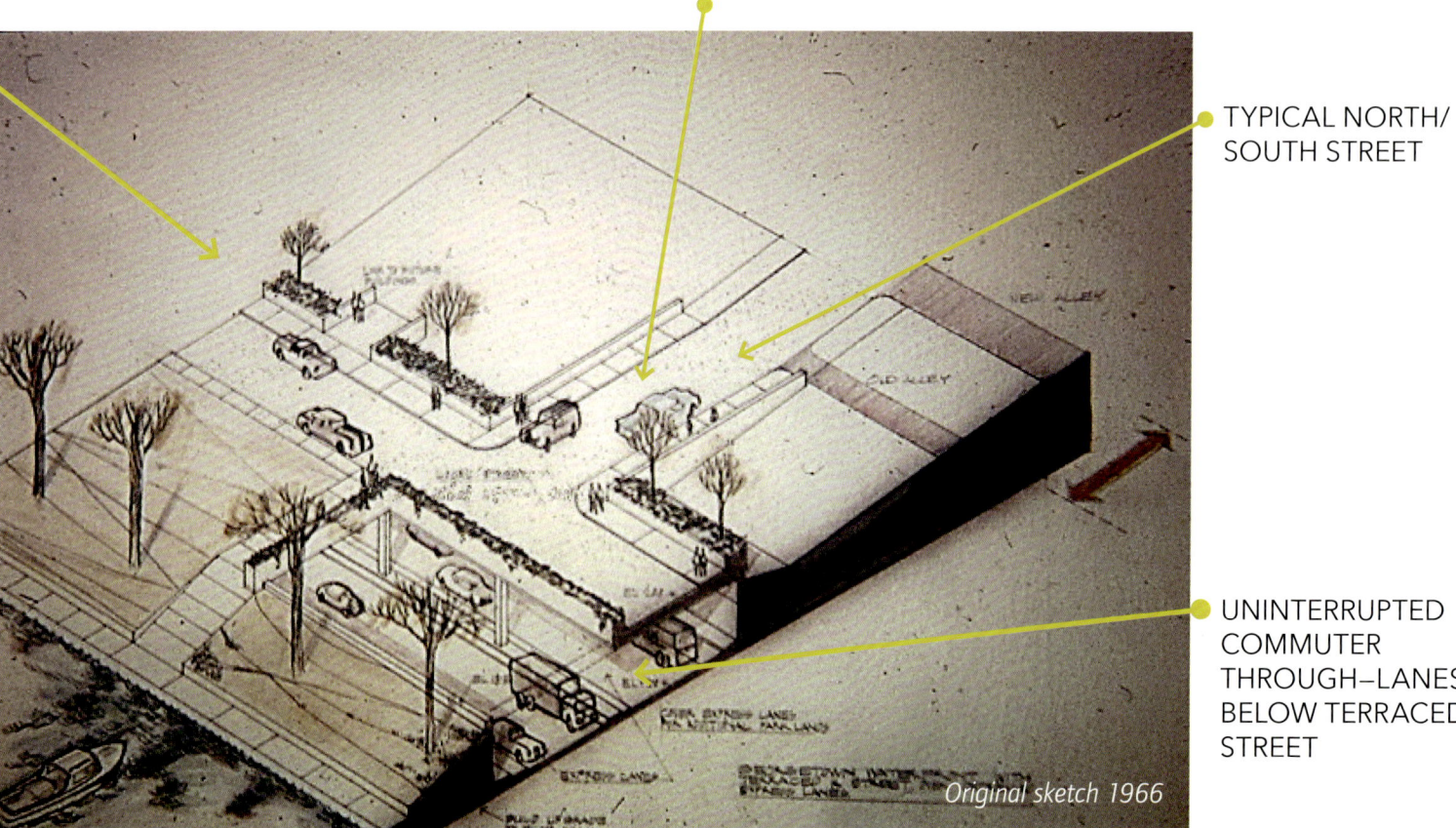

TYPICAL NORTH/SOUTH STREET

UNINTERRUPTED COMMUTER THROUGH–LANES BELOW TERRACED K STREET

Original sketch 1966

Feasible at the time, one way of removing the Whitehurst Freeway would allow through-commuter traffic. This scheme was transmogrified by NCPC consultants into a too-expensive $200 million tunnel.

HOW TO REPLACE THE WHITEHURST FREEWAY

Existing conditions at Key Bridge and the Whitehurst.

SPIRAL RAMP FROM KEY BRIDGE

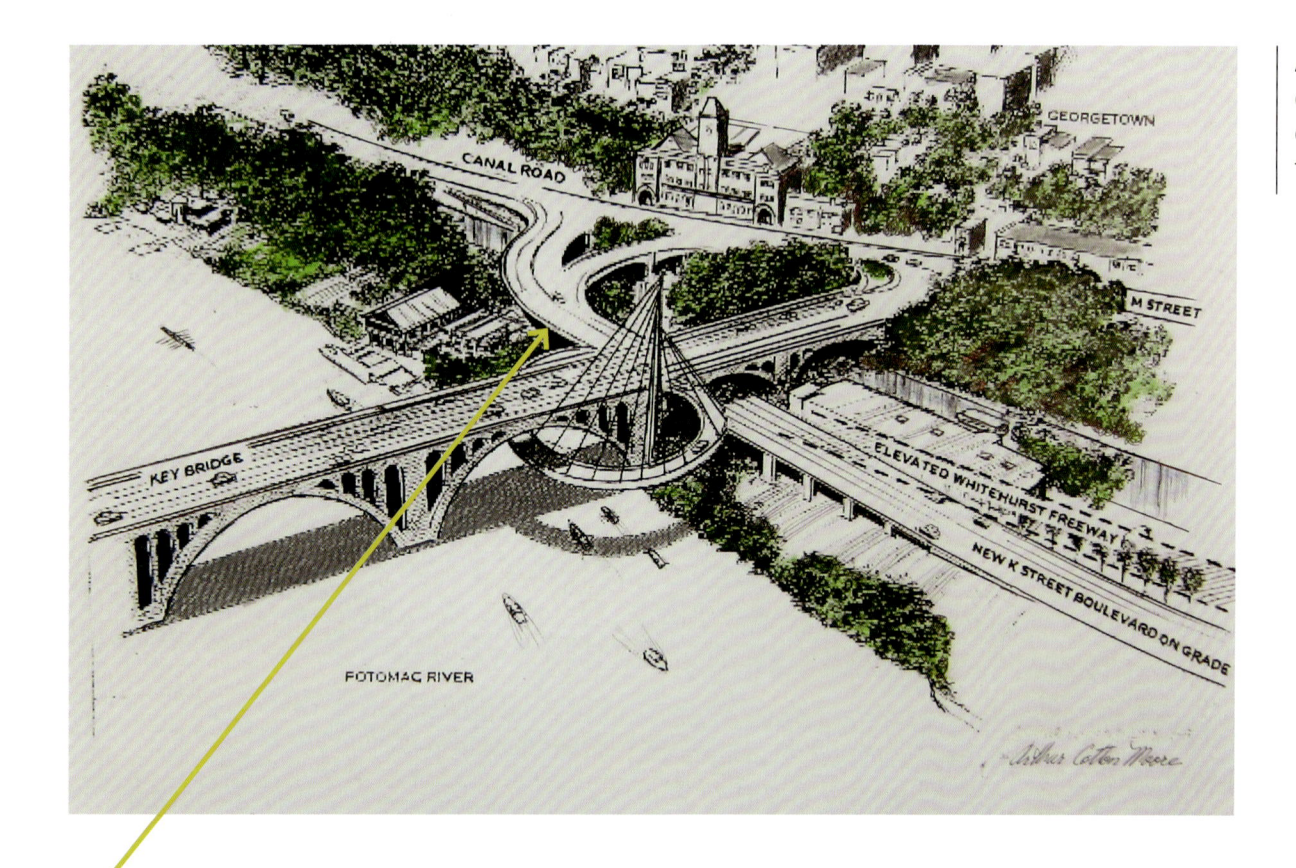

A spiral ramp would permit eastbound Key Bridge commuter traffic to descend to an on-grade boulevard.

Reused end section of the freeway, which connects to M Street and passes under the Key Bridge arch, sloping to grade.

GEORGETOWN

2 AIRPORTS: RONALD REAGAN (NATIONAL) + WASHINGTON DULLES INTERNATIONAL

REPLACE NATIONAL AIRPORT WITH A NEW TOWN, AND A FAST RAIL LINE TO DULLES

We protested a plan to enlarge National Airport, and proposed replacing the dangerously-short runway airport with a new town. The expansion was stopped; however, the same pressures for enlarging (now) Reagan Airport still exist.

We also proposed a rail line to underused Washington Dulles International—an idea that is partially completed as of 2017.

Washingtonian magazine (March 1967)

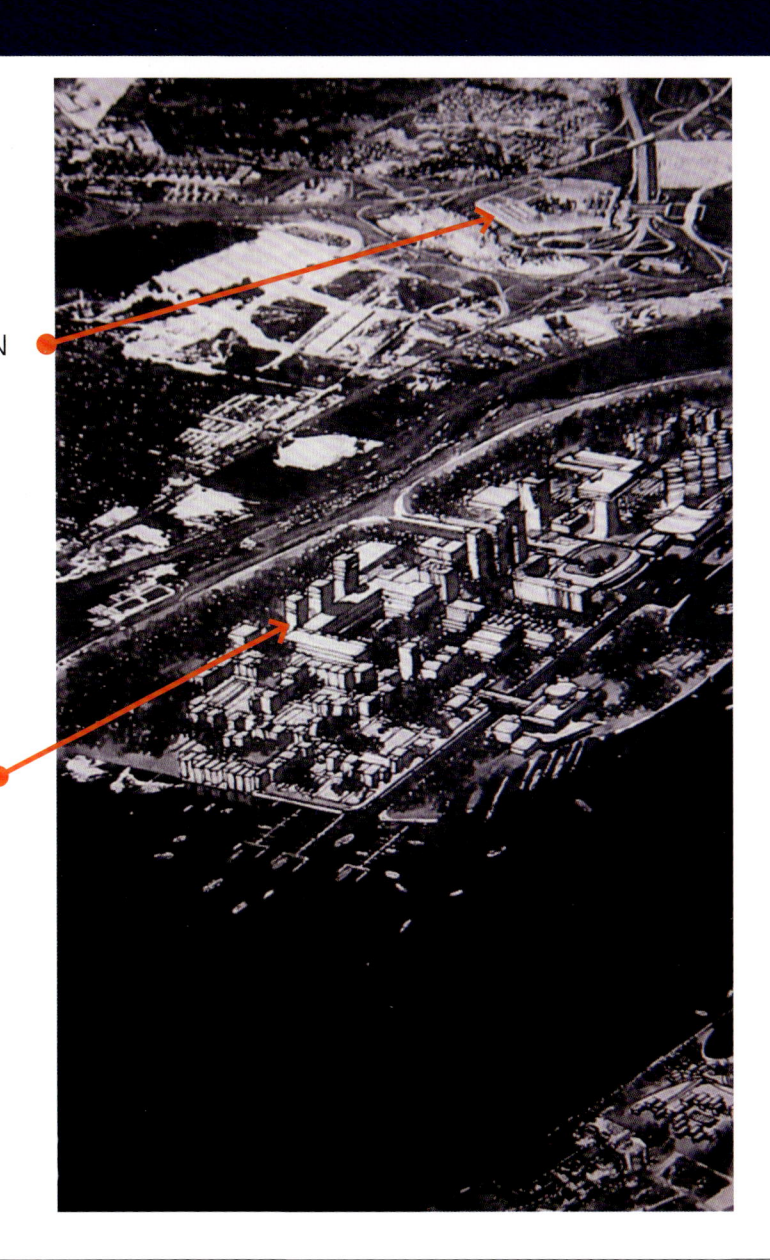

PENTAGON

NEW TOWN

Our Nation's Capital: *Pro Bono Publico* Ideas | proffered by ARTHUR COTTON MOORE FAIA ©

A ROSSLYN AIR TERMINAL FOR DIRECT BUS/MOBILE LOUNGE CONNECTION TO AIRPLANES

Our solution to facilitate access to Dulles was to create a Rosslyn Air Terminal, which would make National more dispensable, by adapting buses to mate with airplanes, like mobile lounges.

This sketch shows a mobile lounge on the left and a specially designed double-decked bus on the right, both filling a soon-to-depart plane with passengers and baggage. The bus has come directly from the air terminal building to hook-up directly with the plane, thus bypassing going through the airport proper. The coming jumbo-sized planes could thus be boarded efficiently and simultaneously by lounges from the Dulles terminal and the buses from the air terminal building in Rosslyn. In effect, then, the fifty bus platforms in Rosslyn can be taken as fifty new departure gates to those already at Dulles — an immediate doubling of Dulles's capacity.

PUBLISHED IN:

Washington Post (August 1967 and November 1996)
Congressional Record (September 1967)
Esquire magazine (June 1968)
Progressive Architecture magazine, in a retrospective review of our work (July 1973)

AIRPORTS

THE ROSSLYN AIR TERMINAL

Basically, the air terminal building is a round structure enclosed by a raised traffic ring with ramp connections feeding directly from the Theodore Roosevelt Bridge; ramp connections to the George Washington Parkway; Route 66 serving Dulles; and Route 50 as the phase-out connection to National. The plan yields a direct route from Washington via Constitution Avenue, or the inner loop and the E Street Expressway. Also shown is the path of a possible rapid transit line which would run in the median of Route 66, beginning and ending under the last parking level of the terminal building at a circular platform around the elevator core. Also suggested is a possible transfer point from the proposed subway line which would tie the project into the Greater Washington Transit System.

The close-up of the terminal shows the raised traffic ring with its connections to the Theodore Roosevelt Bridge and Route 66/Dulles Highway. The traffic ring contains about 800 short-term parking spaces. Traffic to long-term parking, taxi loading, pickup and dropoff, and bus loading, simply comes around the ring and loops into the building and out again on special levels, and back into town — all on one-way non-crossover flow. Not shown, but inside the building, is a continuous, easy ramp containing over 2,000 long-term, self-park spaces, each within a maximum distance of eighty weather-proof feet to the elevator shaft (black spine), which takes the traveler directly to the ticket counters, baggage check-in, and bus-loading floor. At this point — the ticket counter — the trip and airlines' responsibility begin for baggage, connections, and you, the passenger. The airlines would then be dealing with point-to-point transportation, and the ride to the airport would become as much a part of the trip as the plane ride. Ultimately, rapid transit could be brought in at a loop at the lowest level; passengers then could check in, take the elevator down to the trains' circular loading platform, and be at Dulles in a matter of minutes. The local area governments and Park Service ought to give immediate thought to setting up a trans-government agency, like a port authority, to build and run the terminal. The Federal Aviation Administration and the airlines ought to be delighted with the inexpensive escape hatch from the accelerating problems of National Airport.

3

THE JOHN F. KENNEDY CENTER FOR THE PERFORMING ARTS

The Washington Post

Get Down by the River, Washington

Build some steps and hop on a ferry.

Unlike so many grand schemes for Washington, here is a little plan for the capital's emerging new personality as a river-front city. It involves extending a waterfront walkway, building a dock and getting a ferry boat or two or three. Ferry service, which has given new life to Boston, New York and Seattle, could bring pleasure to the public and even relieve our clogged bridges.

Today the Potomac divides Maryland and the District from Virginia. But the river, with a ferry service, could unite the adjacent jurisdictions; after all, Fairfax, Montgomery, Prince George's, Arlington, Alexandria and the District all have a common interest in innovative ways to lessen the commuters' burden and in providing more recreation on the water. Most of America's cities have turned their backs on their waterfronts by putting freeways, obsolete industry, railroad lines and a series of barriers between the residents and the water, and Washington is no exception. Few cities in the world have made their river the continuous, bright, breathing edge of city life it should be—only Paris comes to mind. Washington, by building a few steps, could change that. Here's how:

There now exists a successful boardwalk and dock at Washington Harbour. Why not extend that promenade from the new Rosewood Hotel to the bridge next to Thompson's Boat House and continue along the Rock Creek Parkway riverside path? Extending the Georgetown promenade in this way would lead right to two older developments that also border the river but aren't involved with it: the Watergate and the Kennedy Center. The Watergate was conceived as, and clearly wants to remain, a private enclave, but the Kennedy Center is a public building, and its cantilevered terrace extending over Rock Creek Parkway could become a link to the water.

I drew an illustration for this idea a year ago, and I offer it now to the community, particularly the Park Service and the Kennedy Center, which would be responsible for undertaking the project. The illustration shows a landing stretching approximately 180 feet parallel to the river, from which a broad grand stair would rise to bridge the gap to the Kennedy Center's existing terrace between its two fountains. By introducing the first landing, clearance for the parkway would be maintained. The structure would be a simple cantilever, placing almost no weight on the Kennedy Center terrace. Pylons could visually anchor the new grand stair on each side, one of which could contain an elevator for the handicapped. New broad steps could allow Kennedy Center patrons to get closer to the river and would also provide a grandstand where people could sit and watch rowing regattas, or simply the river itself.

Such a landing would link the Kennedy Center not only to the water but also to the commercial vitality of Georgetown. The city would gain a riverside walkway similar to those in Geneva, Paris, Stockholm, Shanghai, Rio de Janeiro and other great cities.

The section between the bridge at Thompson's Boat House and the existing walk in front of the Kennedy Center could even be broadened, perhaps with decorative paving, more lighting and a separate bike path.

The new Kennedy Center waterfront connection would be a logical place for another set of stairs at the sea wall leading to a floating dock, where ferries, cruise boats and water taxis could stop. A trip to the theater from Alexandria by ferry could be quite a romantic switch from the usual hassle of traffic and parking.

The idea wouldn't have to cost much. The Georgetown Waterfront Arts Commission has already endorsed the concept and has even offered to raise the funds for construction. Preliminary reactions from the Kennedy Center and the Park Service have also been very positive.

Properly done, the steps and promenade could look like they had always been a logical part of the master plan for the Kennedy Center; in fact, the first aborted scheme for the Kennedy Center even contemplated a connection to the river, but in an entirely different way. It could be the right time to revive the idea.

—*Arthur Cotton Moore*
is a Washington architect
who designed Washington Harbour.

THE KENNEDY CENTER STEPS + A LOOP OF FERRYBOAT CONNECTIONS TO VIRGINIA, WASHINGTON HARBOUR, AND THE KENNEDY CENTER

Washington Post (September 1987)

STRUCTURE OF PROPOSED STEPS

A cantilevered stairway to the existing cantilevered Kennedy Center terrace (shown in yellow) places no weight on the existing terrace, or on any part of the center's structure.

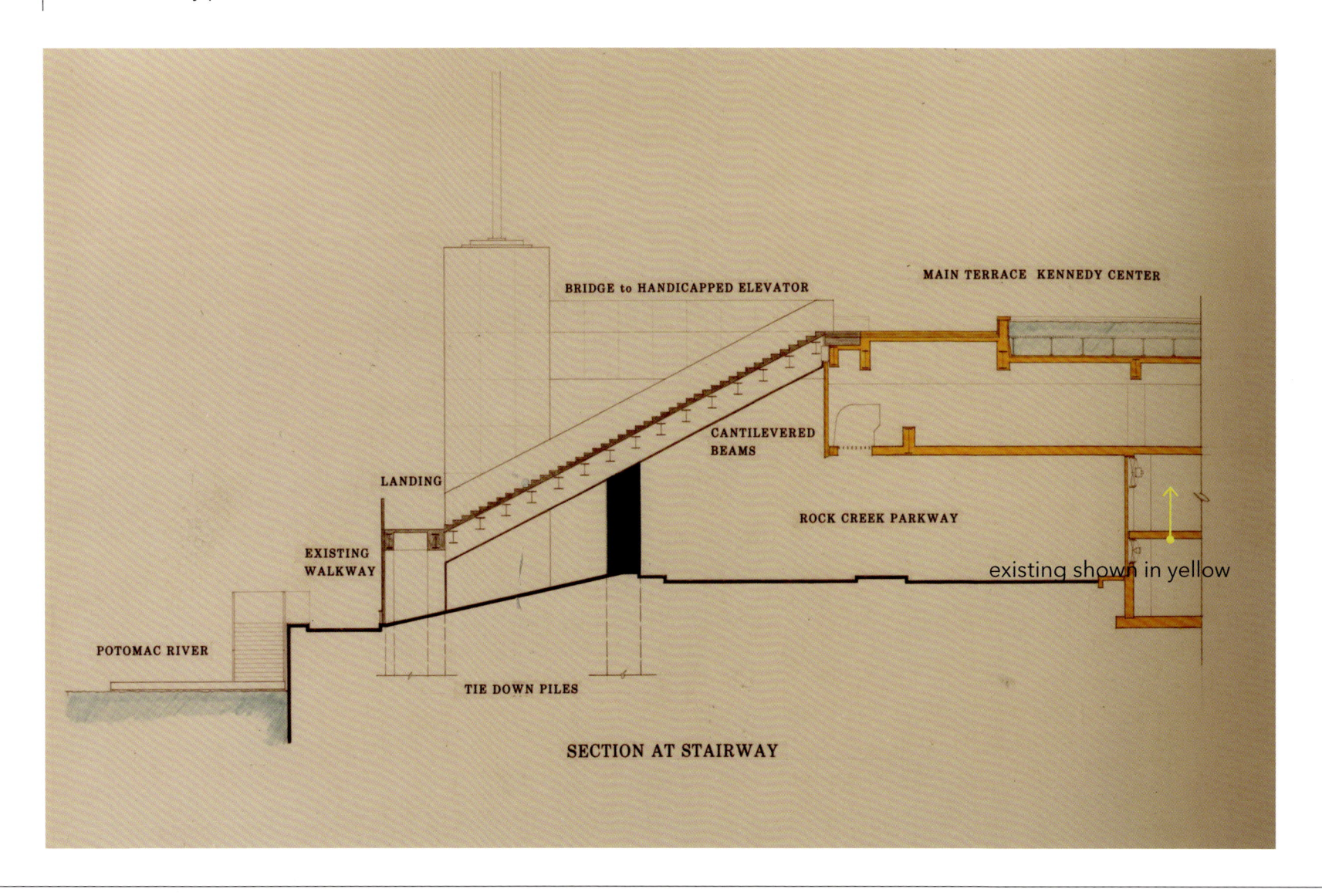

MAIN TERRACE KENNEDY CENTER

BRIDGE to HANDICAPPED ELEVATOR

CANTILEVERED BEAMS

LANDING

ROCK CREEK PARKWAY

EXISTING WALKWAY

existing shown in yellow

POTOMAC RIVER

TIE DOWN PILES

SECTION AT STAIRWAY

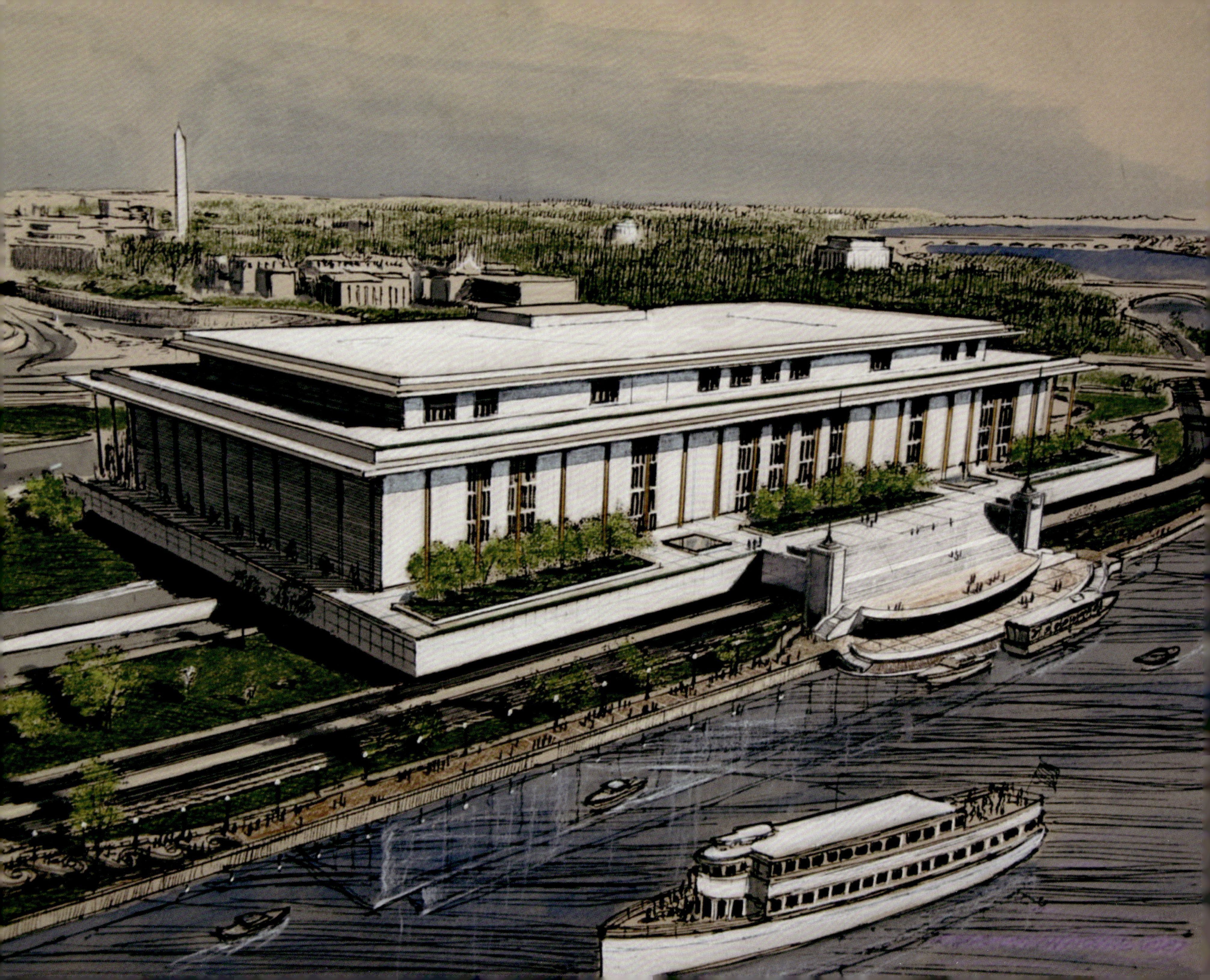

RENDERING OF PROPOSED STEPS

The Kennedy Center Steps, which are buttressed by elevator towers, leading to a ferryboat dock. New terraces over garage additions have created a 1,000-foot-long structure, thereby making the proposed Steps an even more appropriate-in-scale addition, enhancing the Kennedy Center as a memorial to President Kennedy.

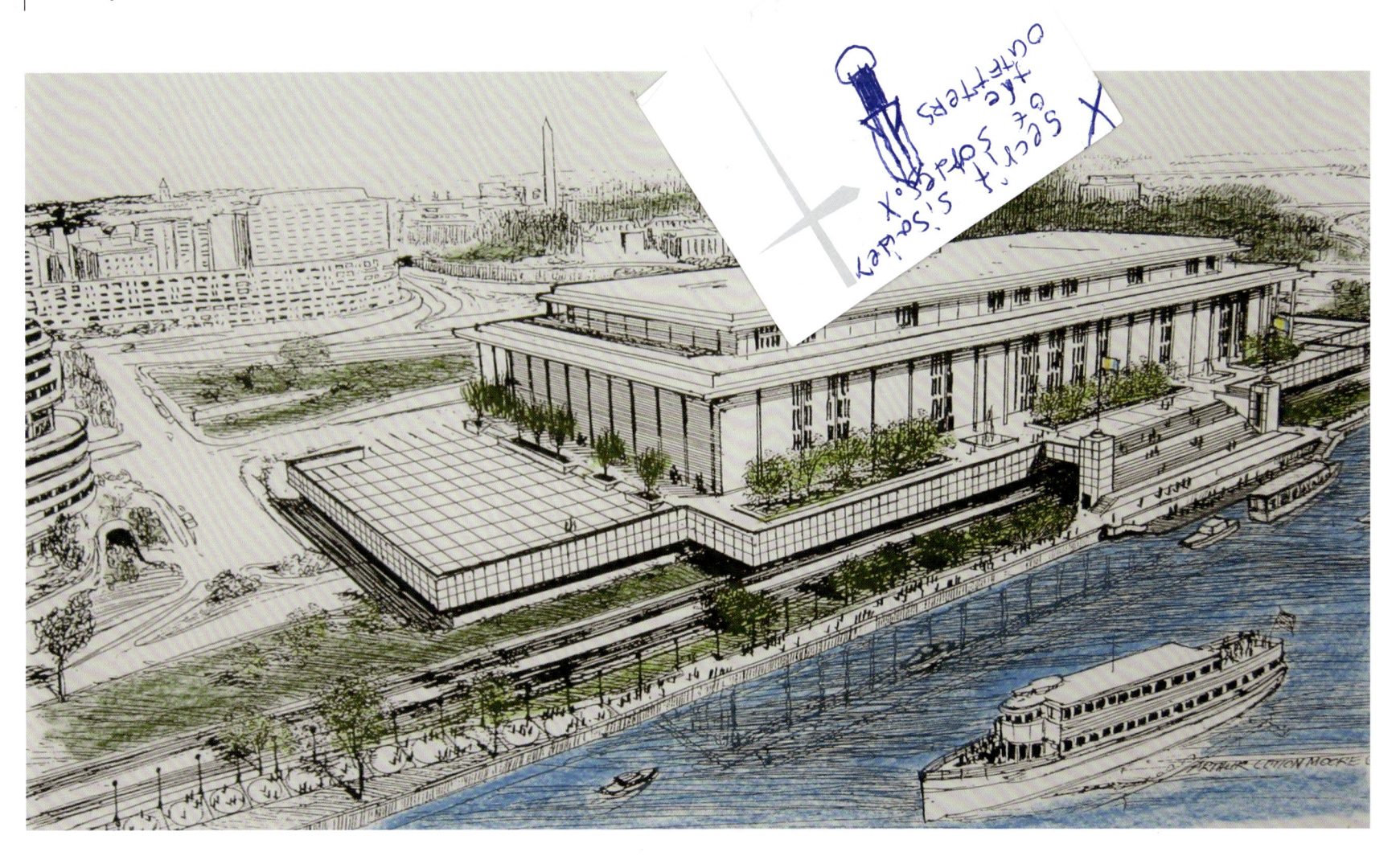

ADDITIONAL PARKING

HARBOURSIDE

WALK DOWN TO KENNEDY CENTER

WATERGATE

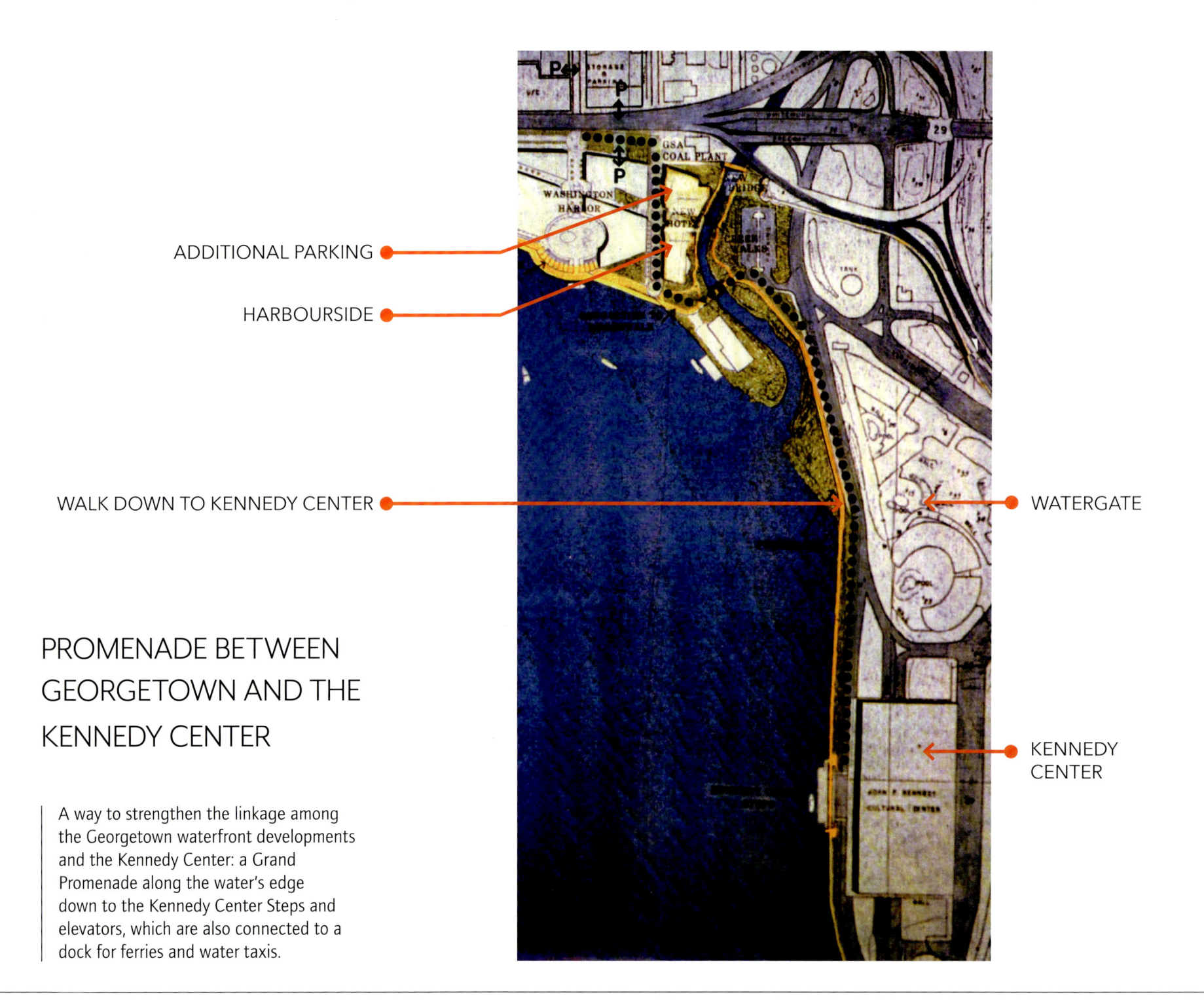

KENNEDY CENTER

PROMENADE BETWEEN GEORGETOWN AND THE KENNEDY CENTER

A way to strengthen the linkage among the Georgetown waterfront developments and the Kennedy Center: a Grand Promenade along the water's edge down to the Kennedy Center Steps and elevators, which are also connected to a dock for ferries and water taxis.

The Promenade, illuminated by Washington Globe and bollard lights, includes decorative paving with a separate bike path. This amenity was partially installed by the National Park Service, but without the lights, benches, decorative paving, or the separate bike path.

CONNECTING ROSSLYN, GEORGETOWN, AND THE KENNEDY CENTER BY WATER

The larger concept is a Ferryboat Loop, linking Rosslyn with Washington Harbour and the Kennedy Center—joining the left bank of the river with its right bank, i.e., Northern Virginia and Washington. This composite shows the dockage comprising the loop. Our idea was endorsed by the nonprofit Rosslyn Renaissance, but at that time was opposed by the National Park Service, because it did not like the addition of a boathouse in Rosslyn.

THE JOHN F. KENNEDY CENTER FOR THE PERFORMING ARTS

4 ALTERNATIVES TO DEMOLITION

SAVING THE OLD POST OFFICE BUILDING

Photograph taken in 1971 by ACM of the blackened and neglected building, two weeks before its scheduled demolition.

BRIDGING THE TWO FACES OF WASHINGTON

LANDMARK POST OFFICE BUILDING

← DOWNTOWN WASH. D.C.

MALL AND SMITHSONIAN →

As shown in this 1971 composite, the building—if we could save it—would be a 24/7 bridge between the two faces of Washington: Our Nation's Capital and the local city.

ALTERNATIVES TO DEMOLITION

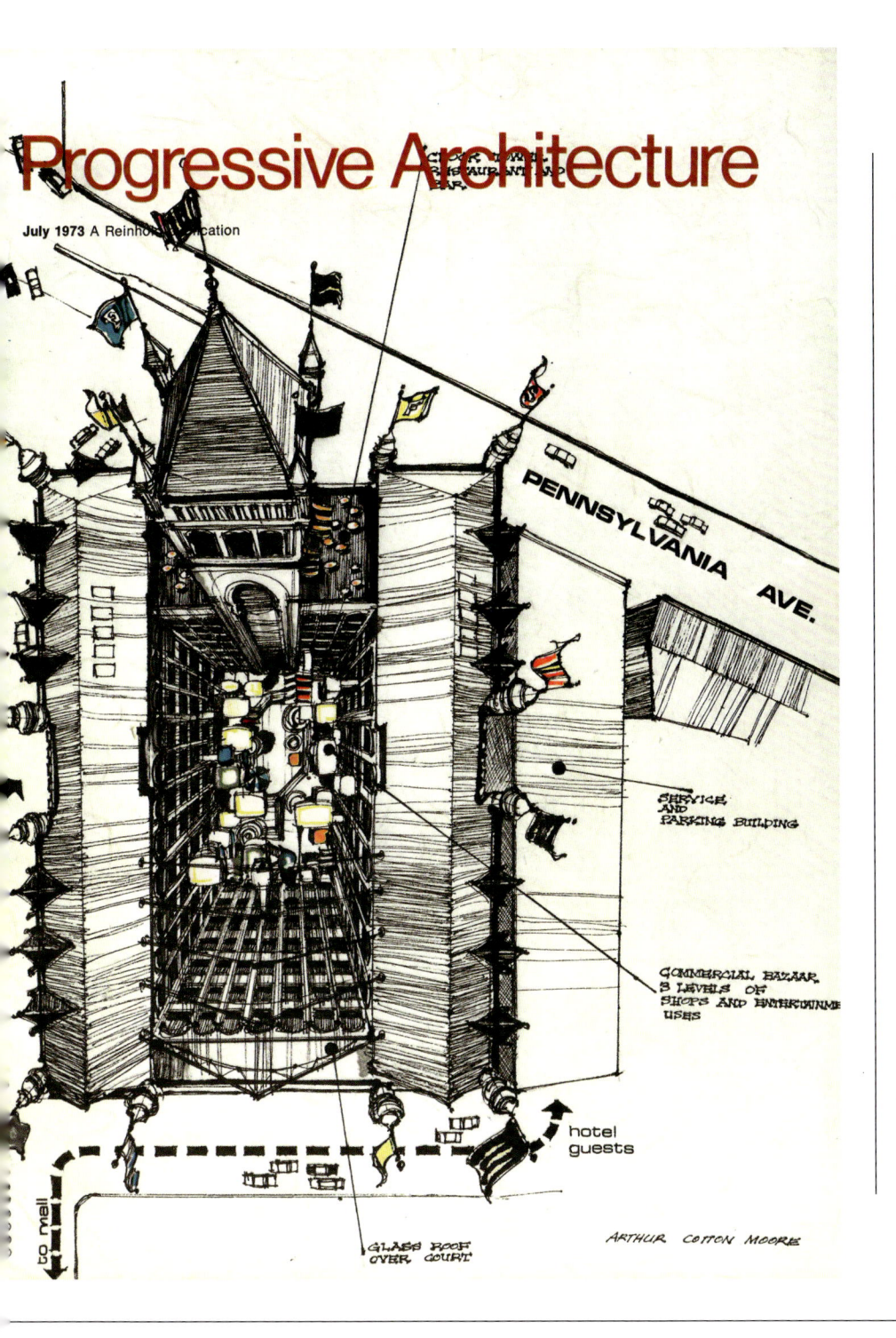

In 1971, we believed our best opportunity to save the Old Post Office was to persuade Congress to deny funding to the General Services Administration for its planned demolition; so we became lobbyists.

Senator Gravel of Alaska was Chairman of the Subcommittee on Public Buildings and Grounds, which had purview. We worked with his office to organize a hearing, and to establish a witness list. We used a personal connection to host a cocktail party so we could meet members of the Subcommittee.

We testified that the building should be a hotel, and we submitted letters of interest from a developer and the president of a national hotel chain, eager to give the building another life. Through the civic-minded generosity of Wolf von Eckardt of The Washington Post, the paper published our plans and sketches. A public demonstration in front of the building followed, mounted by Don't Tear it Down, which we attended.

In the end—just two weeks before the scheduled demolition—the Subcommittee voted down the $400,000 in funds required to demolish the building. (The full story of the OPO is included in our book *The Powers of Preservation*.)

After Nancy Hanks, head of the National Endowment for the Arts, said she would like to be a tenant in the building, GSA then held a national design competition (which we won) to remodel the building. In 2011, GSA held a new competition to design and develop the OPO as a hotel, which we won with The Trump Organization. Due to illness, we left the project soon after. In 2016, the building opened as The Trump International Hotel.

This image is the original 1971 sketch for the *Washington Post*; in 1973, *Progressive Architecture* magazine published a ten page story on our firm, and put the image on the cover.

A PROPOSAL TO SAVE THE THIRD CHURCH OF CHRIST, SCIENTIST

> The church was designed by I.M. Pei Partners. Responding to a request from preservationists, we created a concept and presented it to the Mayor's Agent. Unfortunately, the building was demolished in accordance with a 2010 agreement between the developer and the D.C. Preservation League.

ALTERNATIVES TO DEMOLITION

Our concept would have added office floors above the existing to-be-preserved architectural complex, adding significant new revenue.

Our goal was preservation of the buildings and the key sculptural composition of the church, plus a unique covered-exterior plaza for the city.

SAVING THE L'ENFANT AND McMILLAN PLANS THROUGH ALTERNATIVE SITE PLANNING FOR THE EISENHOWER MEMORIAL

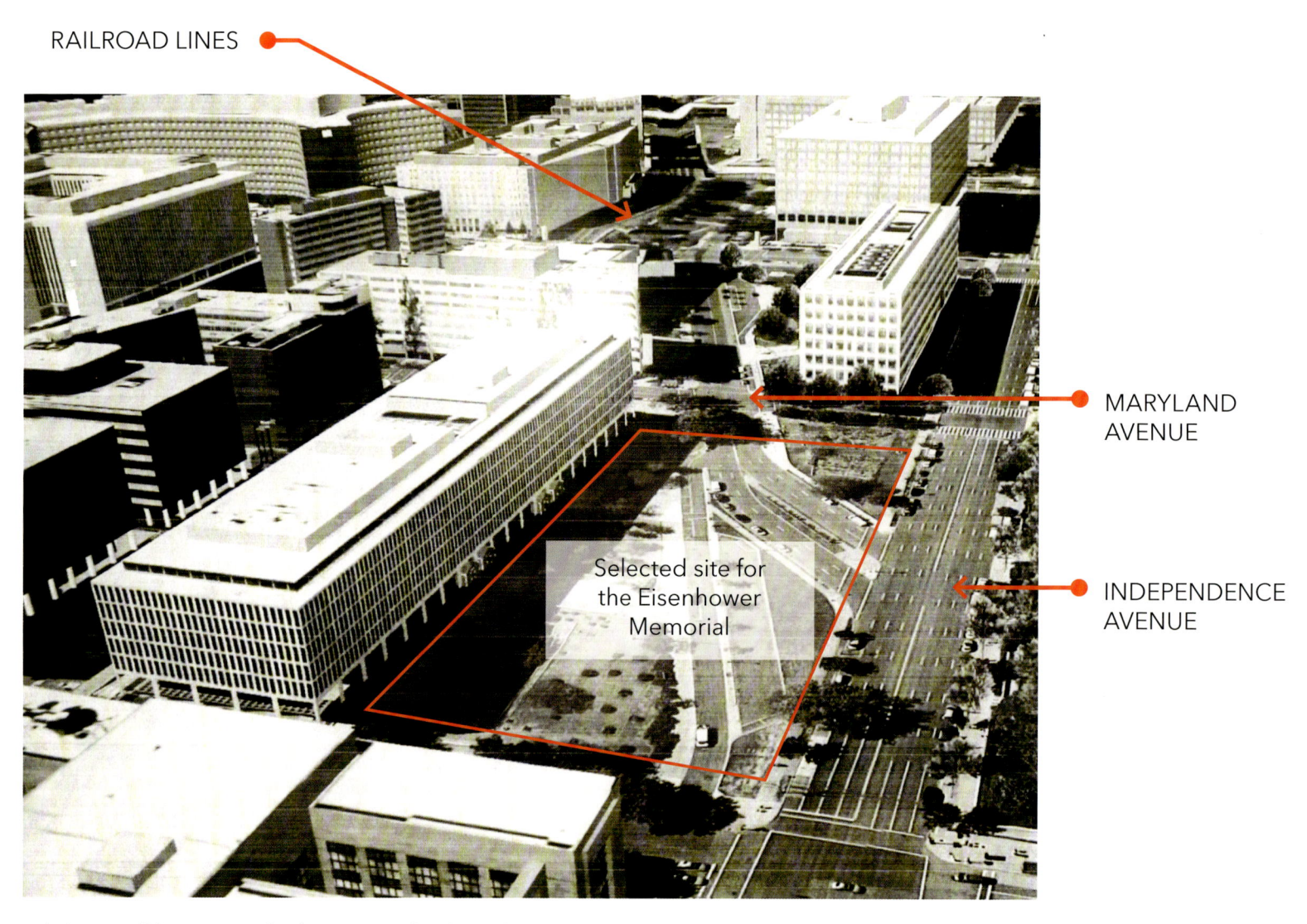

RAILROAD LINES

MARYLAND AVENUE

Selected site for the Eisenhower Memorial

INDEPENDENCE AVENUE

Existing conditions at Maryland Avenue and Independence Avenue.

ALTERNATIVES TO DEMOLITION

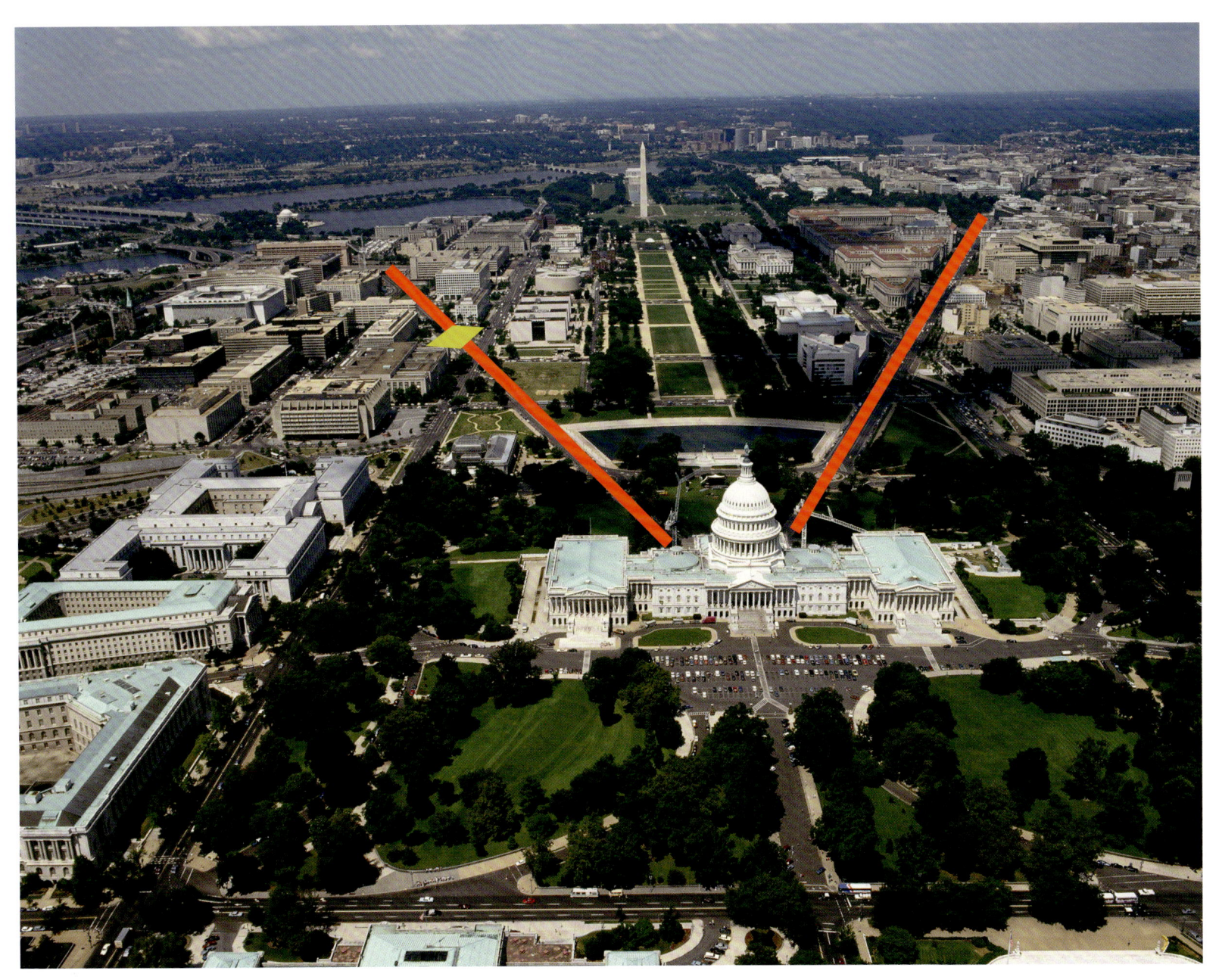

Maryland Avenue and Pennsylvania Avenue are fundamental elements of the historic L'Enfant and McMillan Plans. The Eisenhower Memorial Commission's design severs Maryland Avenue into two parts, thereby permanently destroying the integrity of the historic plans.

A CONTINUOUS MARYLAND AVENUE

Res. 113

MARYLAND AVENUE

In connection with its hearings on the Eisenhower Memorial, the House Natural Resources Committee requested that we present two alternative sites. This alternative divides the site into two parts (Eisenhower as Supreme Allied Commander and as President), which would be joined under Maryland Avenue, just as the National Gallery joins its East and West wings under Fourth Street.

UNDERGROUND MUSEUM CONNECTION

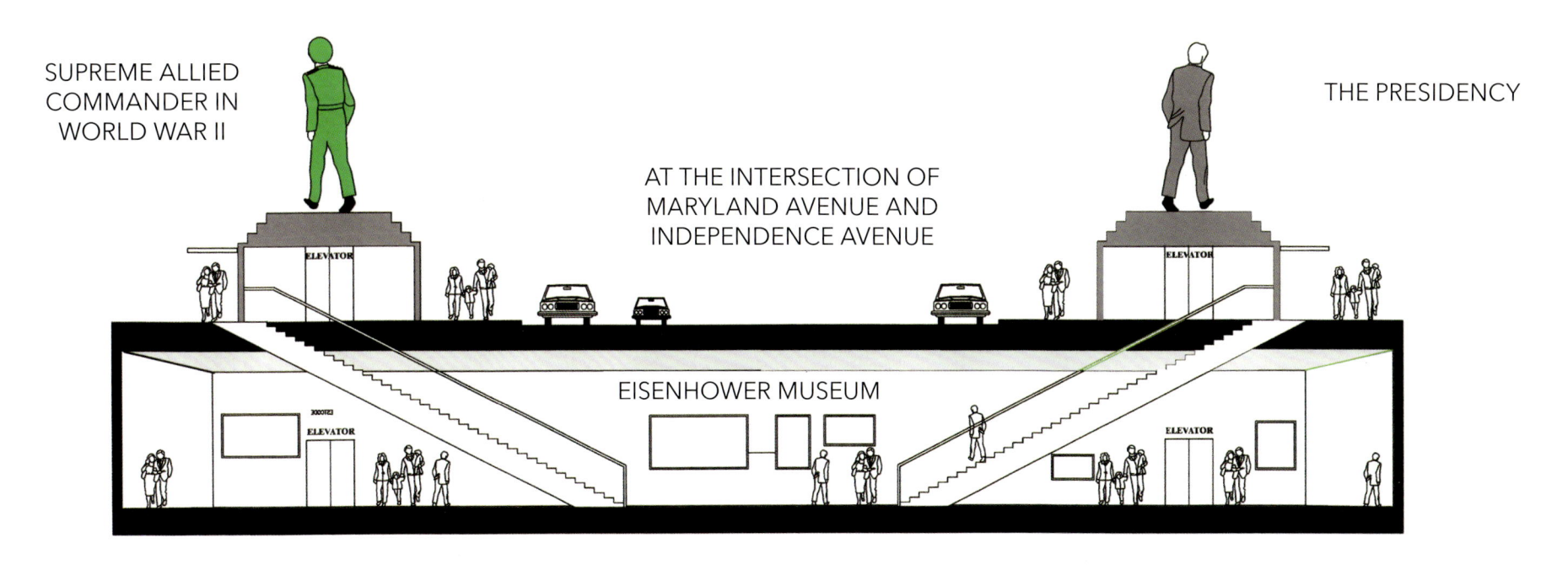

SUPREME ALLIED COMMANDER IN WORLD WAR II

AT THE INTERSECTION OF MARYLAND AVENUE AND INDEPENDENCE AVENUE

THE PRESIDENCY

EISENHOWER MUSEUM

SECTION THROUGH MEMORIAL

(Similar to the connection under Fourth Street joining the East + West wings of the National Gallery.)

Our Nation's Capital: *Pro Bono Publico* Ideas | proffered by ARTHUR COTTON MOORE FAIA ©

A SECOND ALTERNATIVE SITE

A second site alternative near the WWII Memorial would show Ike as Supreme Allied Commander and as President.

ALTERNATIVES TO DEMOLITION

5 THE WHITE HOUSE GROUNDS

RE-OPENING PENNSYLVANIA AVENUE WITH ENHANCED WHITE HOUSE SECURITY

Commentary and Opinion

Window on The President

The closing of Pennsylvania Avenue in front of the White House not only creates a traffic nightmare, but more important, it splits our nation's capital and creates a negative image for our country.

The sense of "bunkerism"—an ever-expanding protective enclave for the chief executive—reinforces the people's feeling that they are becoming isolated from their president. This is supposed to be an open society, but the closing of Pennsylvania Avenue recalls Franklin D. Roosevelt's famous aphorism that "the only thing we have to fear is fear itself."

Americans are well aware of the threat of terrorists after the bombings of the World Trade Center in New York and the federal building in Oklahoma City. But closing Pennsylvania Avenue in front of the White House represents a victory for the forces of lawlessness. France has experienced terrorist explosions throughout its capital city, but the street in front of its presidential palace in Paris has not been closed.

Three measures short of closing the avenue could be taken to protect our president without closing him off from the people. The first would be to restrict truck traffic on that stretch of road. In that way the threat of a truck bomb, such as the one that was used in Oklahoma City, would be eliminated.

The second would be to place handsomely designed guard houses at the corners of 17th and 15th streets NW from which forward observers could monitor traffic.

But perhaps most important would be the installation of a high-tech glass fence—made of a thicker, stronger, more sophisticated version of bulletproof glass—behind the present metal fence already in front of the White House. Tests have indicated that multiple-layer glass can be designed to withstand the blast of hundreds of pounds of TNT.

The installation of a second, somewhat thinner, glass fence about three feet inside the first fence would provide additional insurance against an extraordinarily fierce car bomb, other explosive devices or heavy weapons. The space between the two lines of glass could be planted with decorative shrubs, providing a pretty border to the White House grounds.

Such fences would be expensive, but their cost would fall far short of the cost of the three-block demolition, repaving and relandscaping being contemplated as an "interim" solution to security problems. A "final" monumental replacement of the avenue, as has been suggested in some early proposals, would cost even more.

With a clear, relatively invisible, high-tech glass fence, Americans—who are inseparable from their cars—could once again have that traditional tourist pleasure of driving by their White House, and Washington would become one again.

—*Arthur Cotton Moore* is a Washington architect

President Clinton closed the avenue after the Oklahoma City bombing. The White House fence has been ineffective in preventing jumpers from getting over it; one jumper got into the White House in 2014. Our proposed glass fence would not only protect the mansion from bombs and bullets but would restrict the continuous problem of jumpers to a confined perimeter zone.

Washington Post (February 1996)

GATES ON PENNSYLVANIA AVENUE TO RESTRICT TRUCK TRAFFIC

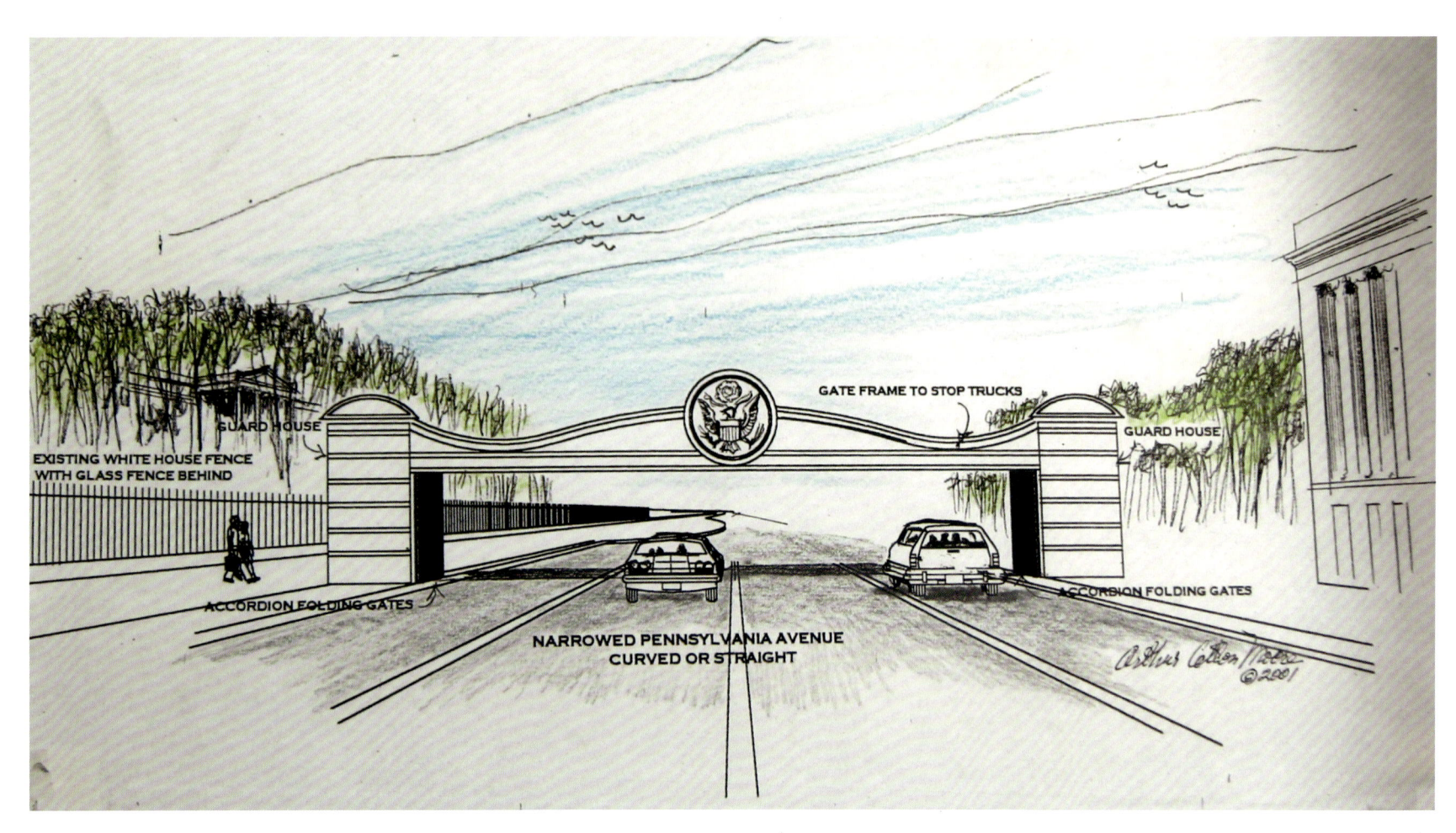

Our idea shows a low gate-frame to prevent trucks carrying explosives from approaching the White House. This would work with proposals by others to curve the avenue, or keep it as it is now, straight.

Washington Star (2001)

CURRENT DEFAULT USE OF PENNSYLVANIA AVENUE IN FRONT OF THE WHITE HOUSE

Skaters on President Thomas Jefferson's declared avenue in front of the White House.

President Jefferson famously said that "kings live in enclaves, but presidents live on streets."

Closed portion of the Grand Avenue is frequently used to park security vehicles.

THE WASHINGTON METROPOLITAN AREA

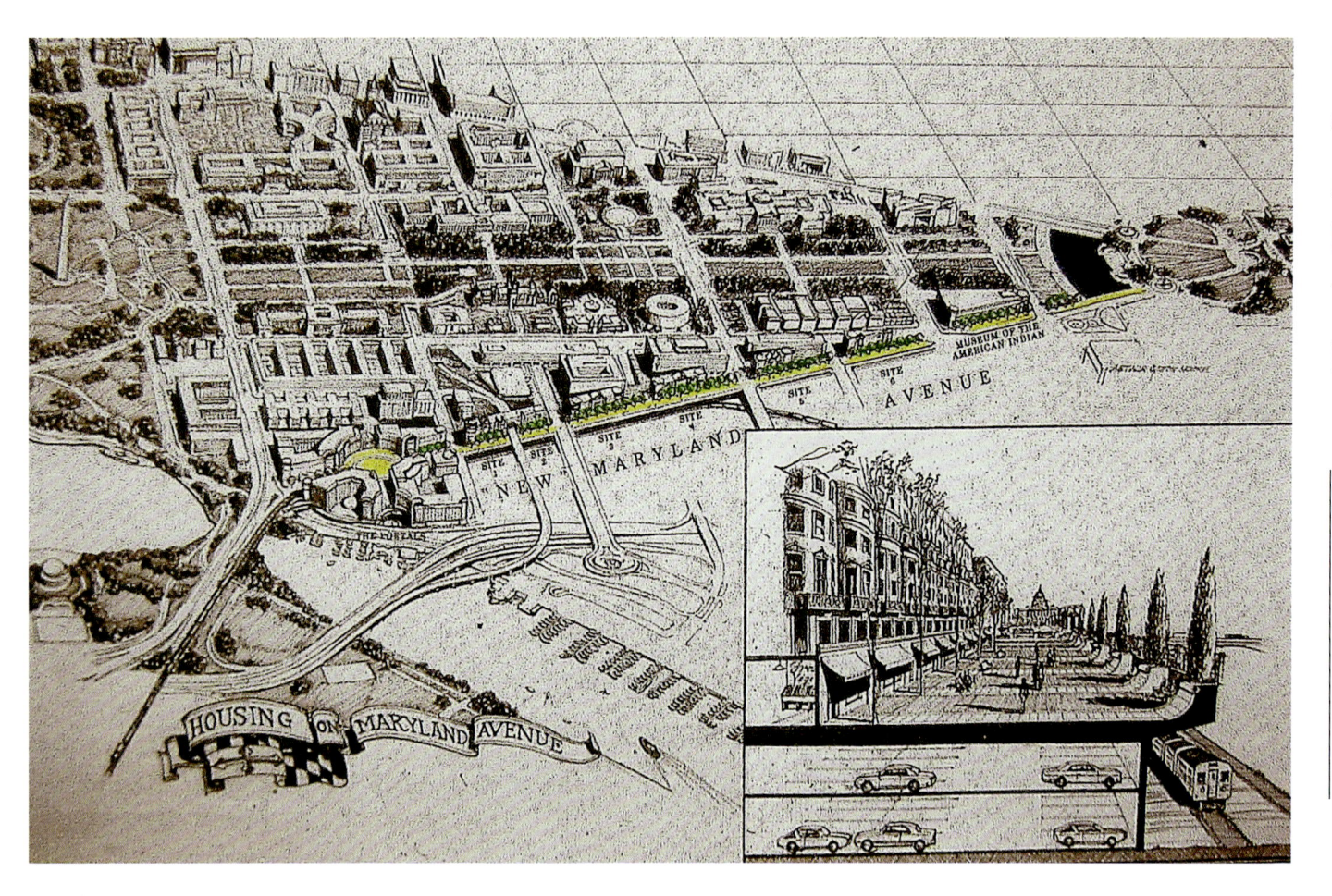

DEVELOPMENT OF MARYLAND AVENUE PURSUANT TO THE L'ENFANT PLAN

Original sketch showing Maryland Avenue, a key element of the L'Enfant Plan. Our idea is that the new, predominately residential buildings, would line the avenue, which could be built above the railroad tracks.

Washington Post (August 1990)

CONCEPTION OF A FUTURE MARYLAND AVENUE TO THE CAPITOL

A photo montage of the development of Maryland Avenue.

Our Nation's Capital: *Pro Bono Publico* Ideas | proffered by ARTHUR COTTON MOORE FAIA ©

An early sketch of a developed Maryland Avenue, showing a scheme of memorial gardens across 14th Street, stepping down to the Tidal Basin.

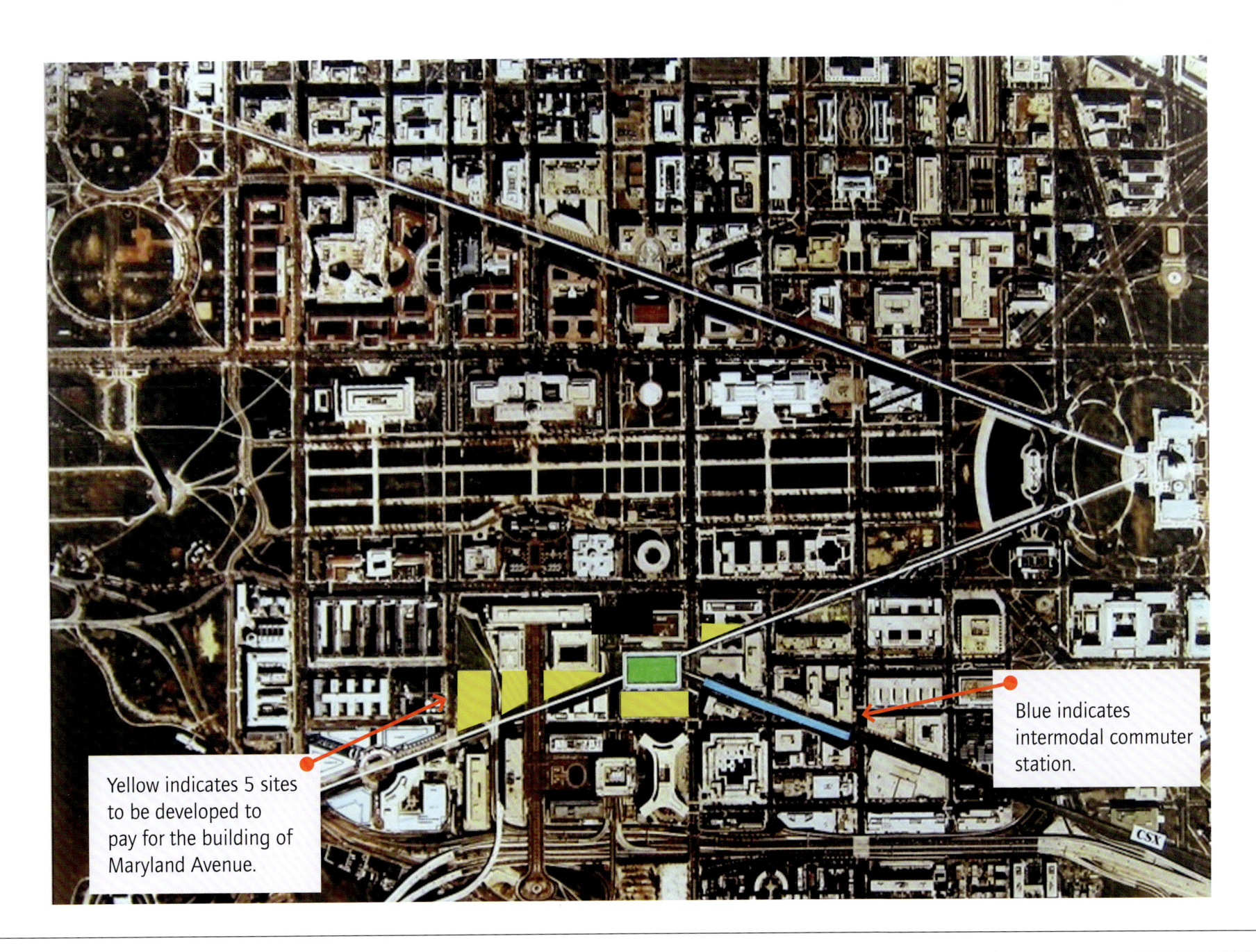

SITES TO BE DEVELOPED

Yellow indicates 5 sites to be developed to pay for the building of Maryland Avenue.

Blue indicates intermodal commuter station.

41 | Our Nation's Capital: *Pro Bono Publico* Ideas | proffered by ARTHUR COTTON MOORE FAIA ©

ONE HUNDRED YEARS LATER

One hundred years after the McMillan Plan (1901–1902) called for the completion of Maryland Avenue, it remains a railroad ditch, except for the block-long section at The Portals.

2001

THE WASHINGTON METROPOLITAN AREA

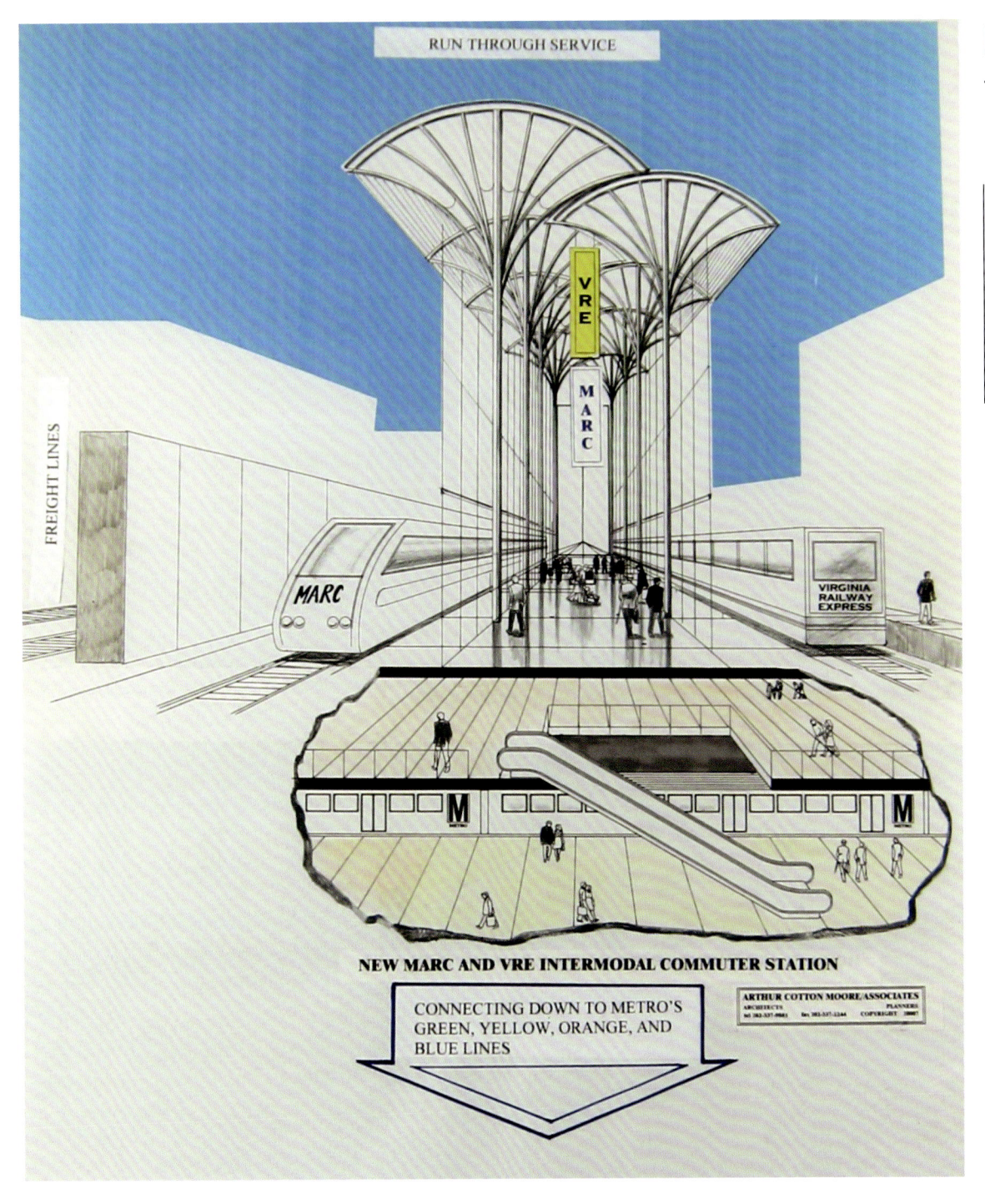

INTERMODAL COMMUTER TRAIN STATION

As part of the development of Maryland Avenue, our idea for an intermodal commuter station at 7th Street and Virginia Avenue would have run-through service for VRE and MARC trains. It would also connect down to four existing Metro lines.

THE NORTHEAST CORRIDOR HIGH-SPEED TRAIN THAT NEVER STOPS

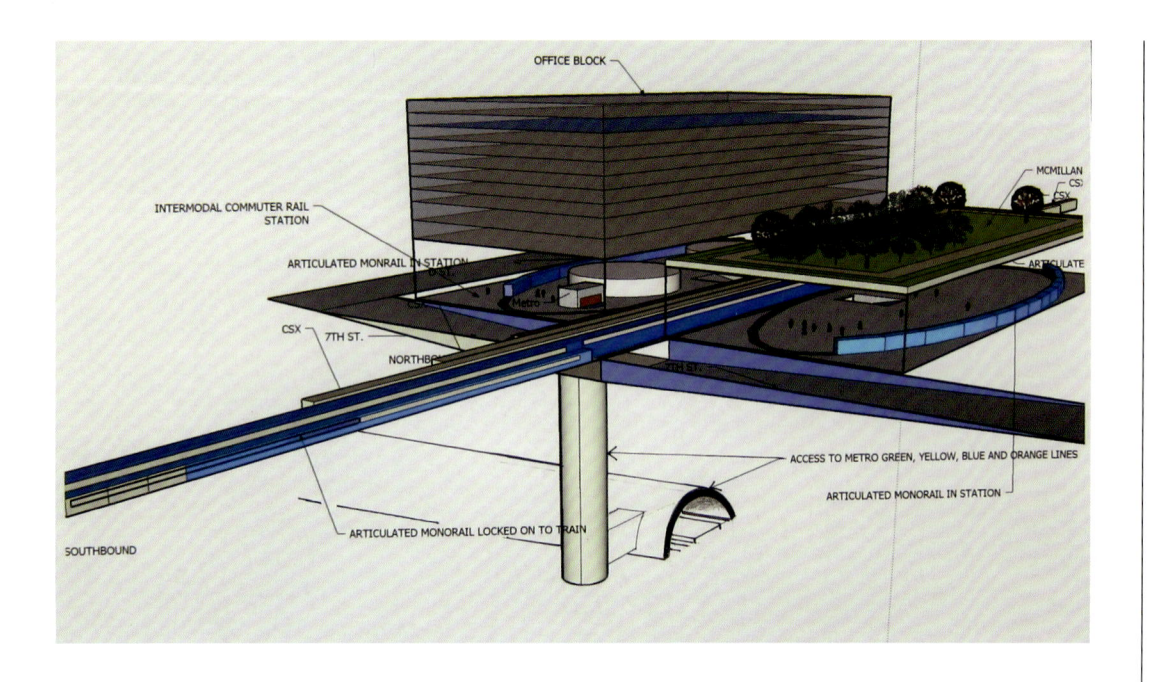

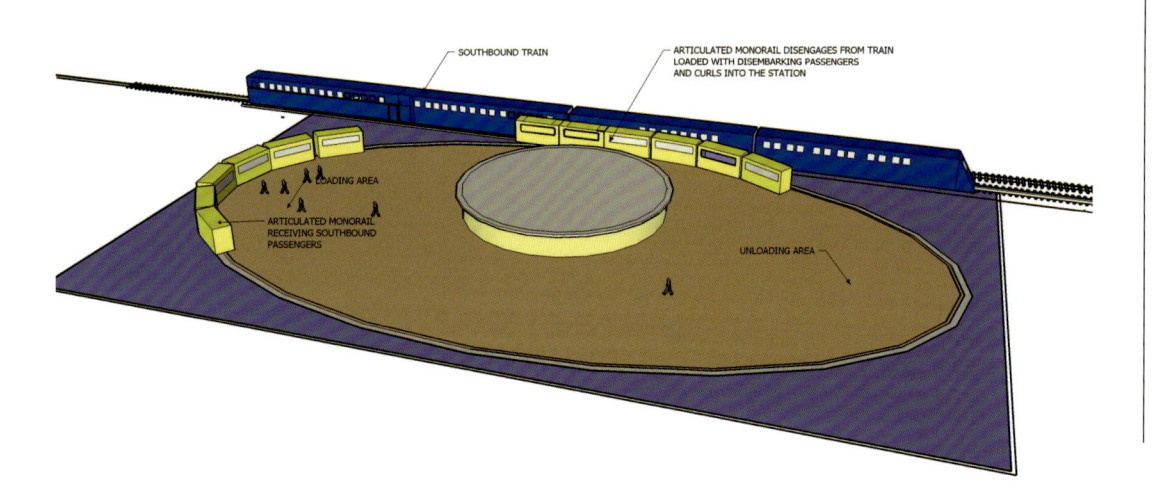

If redeveloped, the site of the GSA Regional Office Building could help to bring to reality the historic McMillan Plan's landscaped square on Reservation 113, by realizing a more compact intermodal commuter station under it, which also gives access to the four existing Metro lines.

Here's how the high-speed train could work: On a signal from an approaching train, a monorail (with passengers wanting to transfer to the main train) speeds up and locks onto the main south-bound train. The passengers get on the main train, and disembarking passengers get on the monorail.

The monorail disengages from the main train and coasts into the station with disembarking passengers. Once empty, the monorail moves to the far side of the station to receive embarking passengers, and then moves to a position to wait for the next train. We think this is the only way to get high-speed train service on the Eastern Seaboard for this reason: Every state would demand a stop, which would result in perhaps a minimum of twelve stops—and probably more—from Boston to Florida. In that program, the train would barely reach full speed before it would have to begin decelerating for the next stop.

THE WASHINGTON METROPOLITAN AREA

GEOTHERMAL ENERGY-SAVING STRATEGIES FOR GEORGETOWN WATERFRONT BUILDINGS, THE WATERGATE, AND THE KENNEDY CENTER

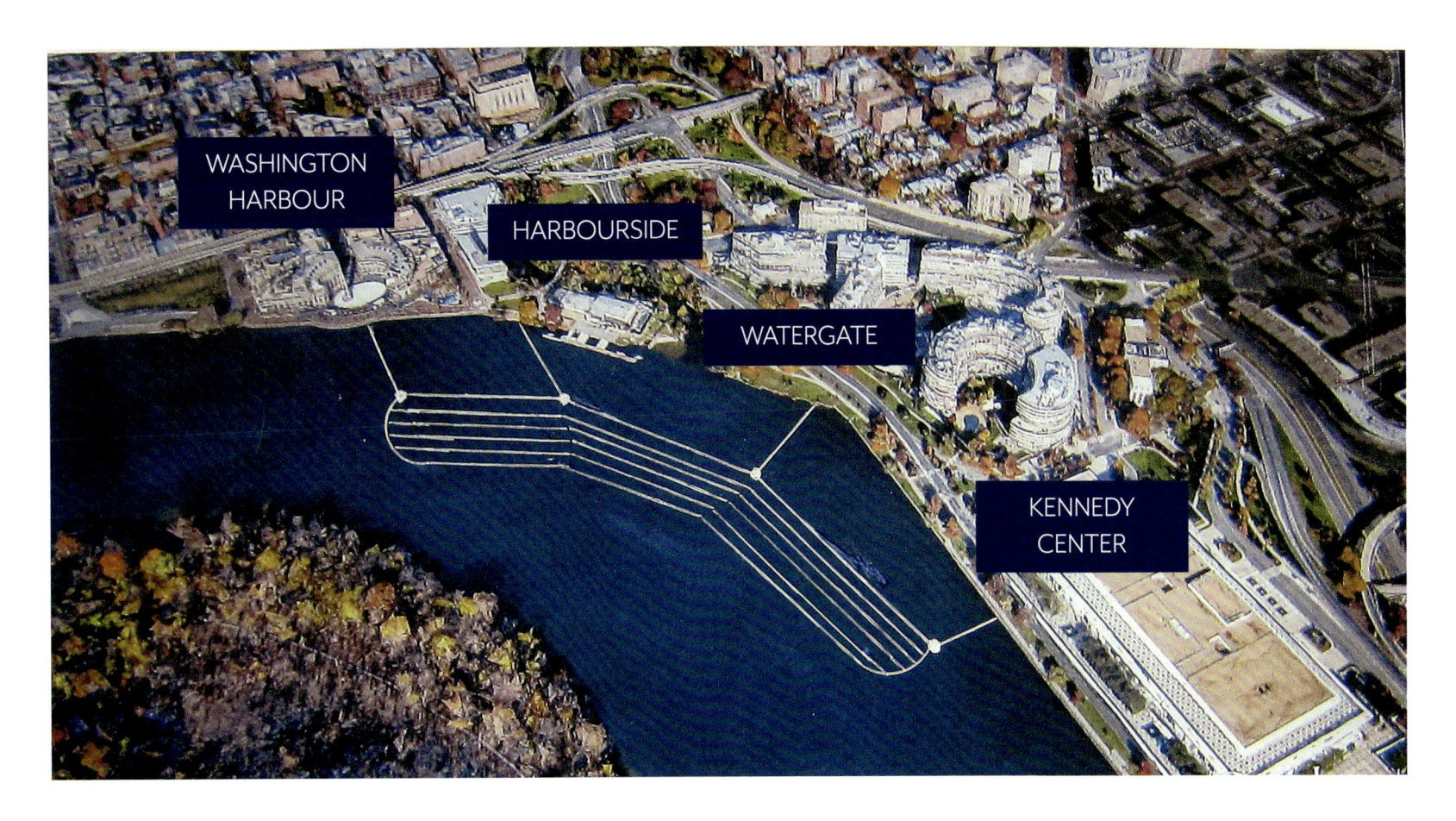

Renewable energy sources—wind, solar, and geothermal—for buildings alongside the river's edge. We secured an extremely fair proposal from the then-SAIC Corporation to study our plan as part of a Federal Government program. Unfortunately, the ownership of the buildings could not agree on SAIC's $10K fee for the study.

SOLAR PANELS ON THE KENNEDY CENTER ROOF

> We had an idea that solar panels on the largest flat roof in town would benefit the Kennedy Center—so we pursued the idea. We introduced the Department of Energy Tiger Study Program to the Center. The DOE study confirmed our assumptions. Despite presidential directives to reduce energy in public buildings, the Center did nothing.

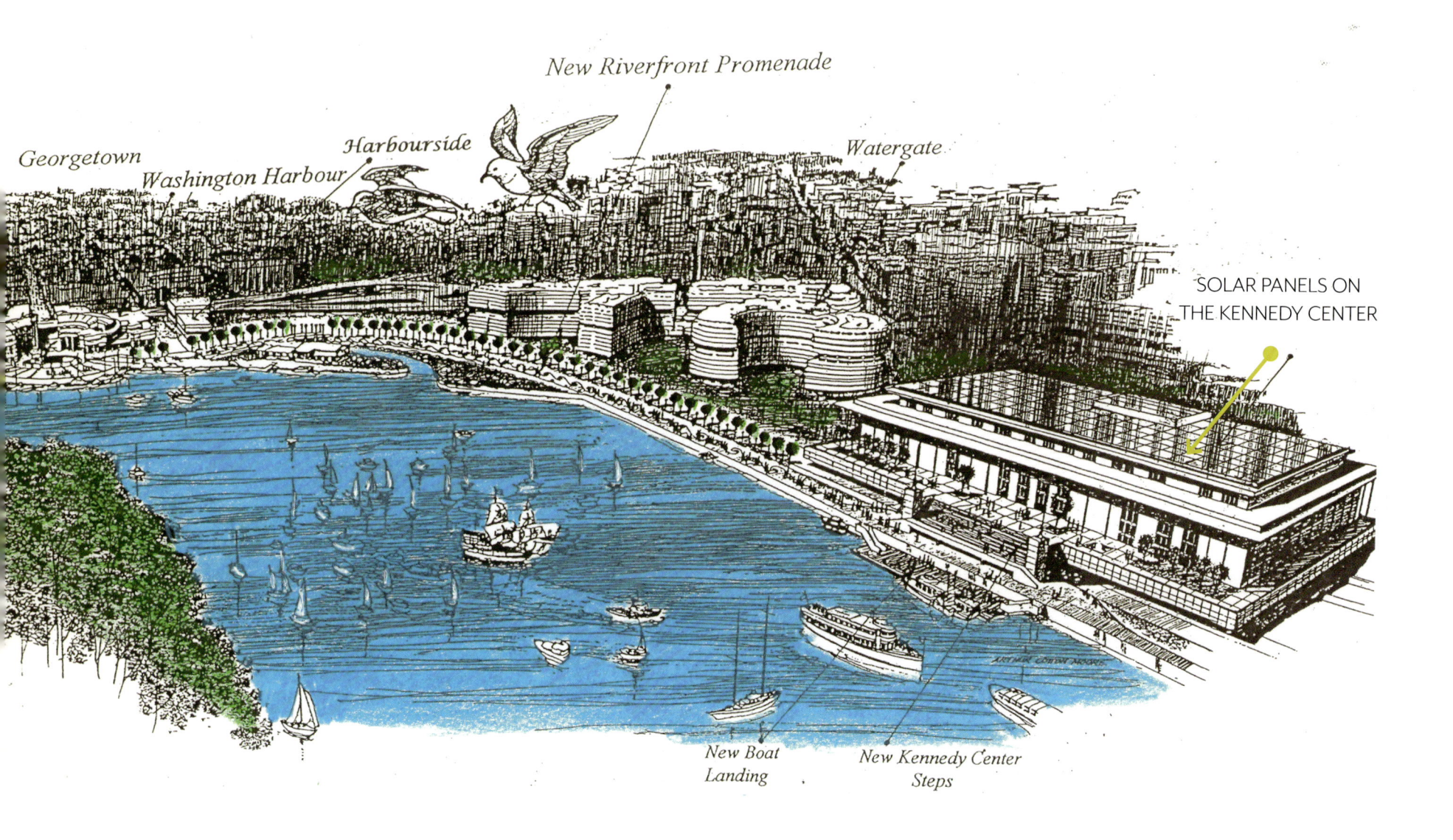

Georgetown — *Washington Harbour* — *Harbourside* — *New Riverfront Promenade* — *Watergate*

SOLAR PANELS ON THE KENNEDY CENTER

New Boat Landing — *New Kennedy Center Steps*

THE WASHINGTON METROPOLITAN AREA

METRO CAR HOUSING FOR OUR HOMELESS POPULATION

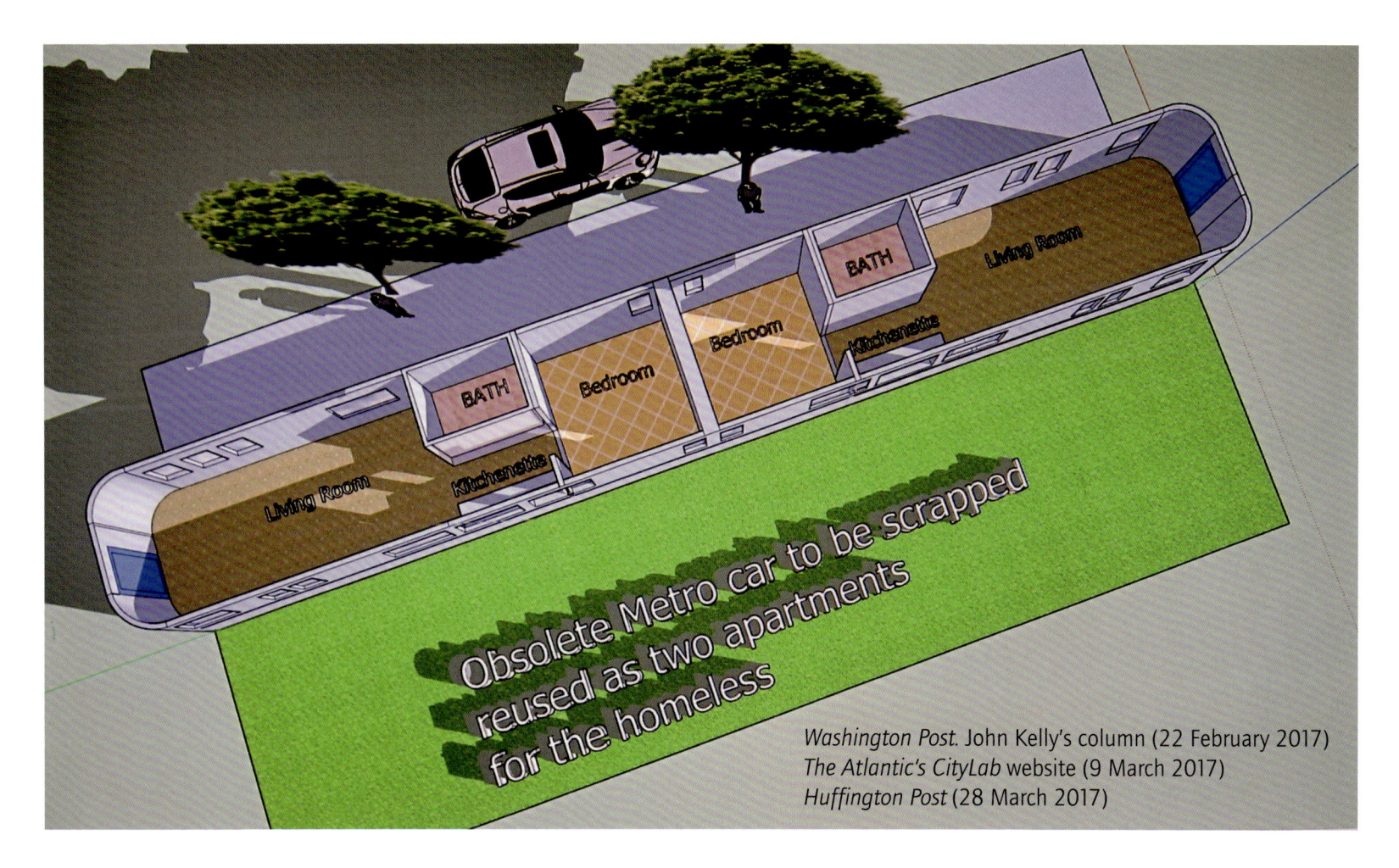

Obsolete Metro car to be scrapped reused as two apartments for the homeless

Washington Post. John Kelly's column (22 February 2017)
The Atlantic's CityLab website (9 March 2017)
Huffington Post (28 March 2017)

Like many cities, Washington has a large homeless population that is largely abandoned. Our mayor's solution was to enter into expensive leases with private developers, at the end of which—after spending millions of dollars—the city would have nothing. As Metro receives its new cars, it actually pays to turn its old cars into scrap. Moved by the waste, our idea was this: The city should acquire the discarded cars, and remodel/furnish and divide them into two one-bedroom, 560-square-foot apartments for our homeless citizens. Recycling them as housing would cost less than a tenth of new construction, and would yield significant savings over the city's current expensive homeless program.

Here's how the idea could work: The cars are watertight aluminum enclosures with built-in windows; they are heavy and aerodynamic enough to withstand strong winds. Four concrete footings would be poured so the wheels could be welded to a series of anchor bolts. Kitchenettes and bathrooms (a shower/toilet/sink) would be prefabricated units. On the roof of each car would be solar panels for hot water and electricity, providing power for a thru-wall unit for heating and cooling. Each car would be self-sufficient except for water and sewer hookups. The connecting doors between train cars would serve as the front door to each apartment.

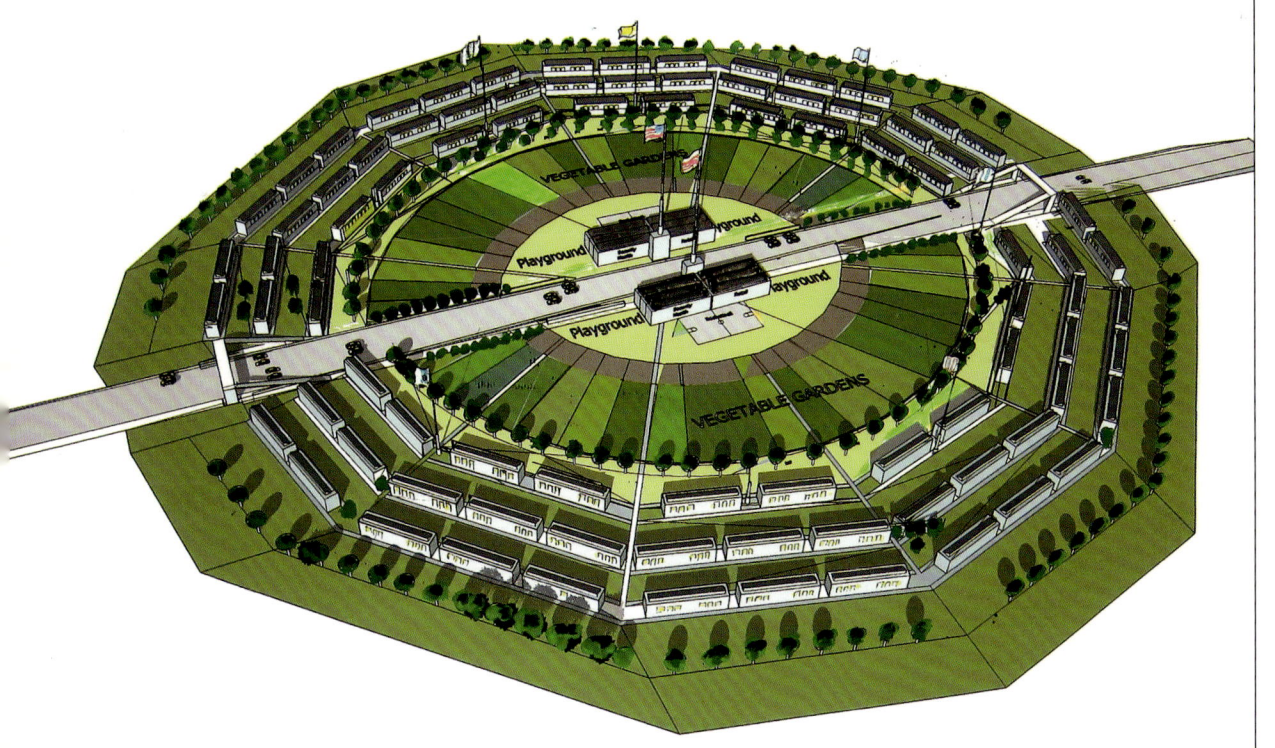

The response to this idea was such that we felt obliged to extend our plan toward an optimum implementation (however much of a dream that might be).

We focused on RFK Stadium as the site for these reasons: The city leases it from the federal government. No sports team wants it. A Metro stop is right there, and it has adjacent land for development of affordable housing—another dire need of the city. Further, the McKinney Homeless Assistance Act allows for offering underutilized federal real estate for homeless development. Another alternative site owned by the District which also is near a Metro, is land north of the new hospital on the east side of St. Elizabeths, which has no adjacent residential area.

Conceptually, this all-inclusive, eighty-six-car, 300-to-400-person housing development comprises playgrounds, a medical clinic, social services, dining rooms, classrooms, gyms, administrative offices and laundry rooms. It also includes vegetable and flower gardens/greenhouses, to create a co-op. Residents would get a home with a key to their front door, and the privacy, safety, and dignity they deserve.

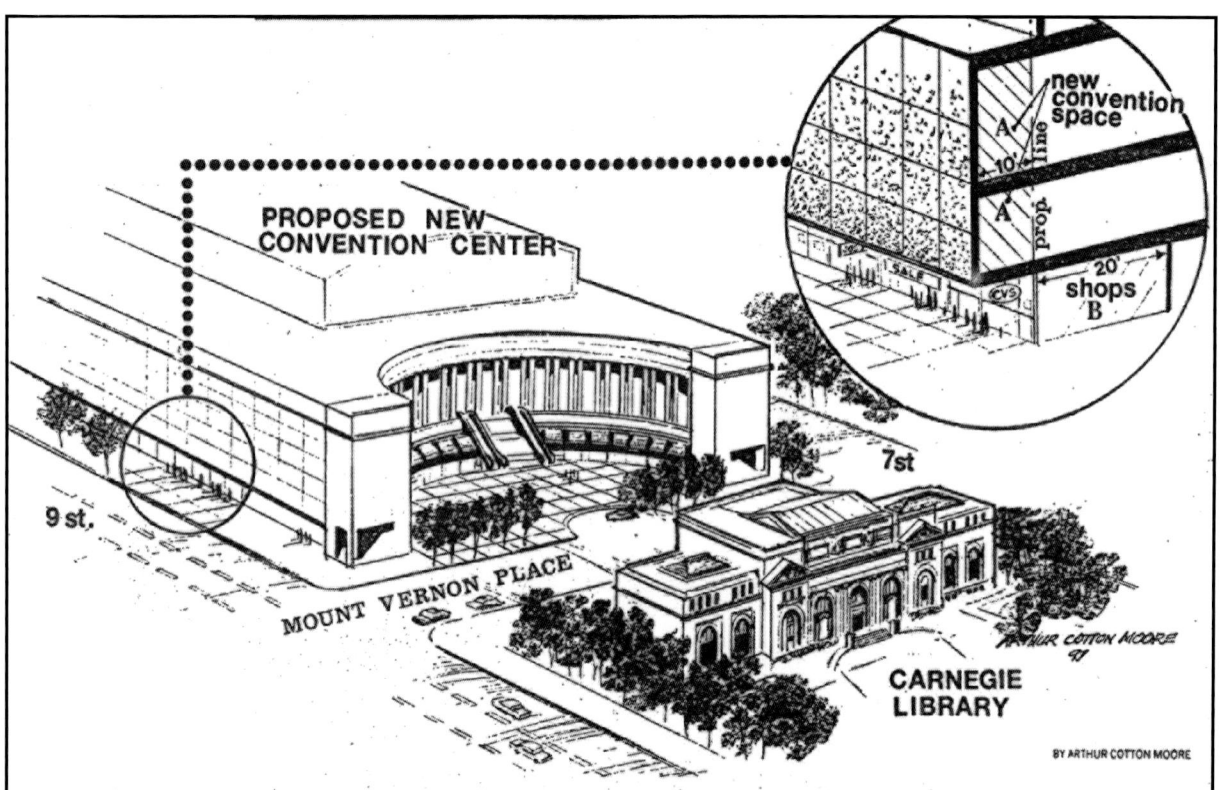

SUGGESTIONS FOR THE NEW CONVENTION CENTER

... Design changes to humanize a behemoth of a building

Washingtonians who have been impressed by the large but rather austere bulk of the convention center now can look forward to a new structure downtown that will make the present one look like a charming miniature.

Washington's new convention center will occupy six city blocks and offer the surrounding community the prospect of a largely blank, 115-foot-high facade. I would like to make two suggestions of what to do about all this blank canvas.

First, under the present design proposal, the south end of the new convention center design will be a large open box devoted mostly to circulation, but it will be expensive to heat and cool. Why not replace it with a plaza, which would provide a handsome city-scaled entrance? A plaza also would provide a breathing space for the landmark Carnegie Library, which sits directly across the street. The current convention center design will be visually crushing for the library. I envision a semicircular plaza, which is a motif characteristic of the Eighth Street axis, but the plaza could take any shape.

Second, on the remaining facades along Ninth, N and Seventh streets NW, I suggest a trade-off so that all that community-killing blankness can be avoided. A few token retail outlets in the present proposal will do little to alter the fortress-like appearance of the proposed convention center, but planners resist devoting any additional space to retail because size is a determining factor in many convention bookings and any loss in square footage may mean a loss of business.

Nevertheless, the surrounding commercial and residential community has a critical need for streets animated by retail life. This could be accomplished without a sacrifice of convention business through a plan that has worked well elsewhere.

The upper two stories of the mainly three-story convention center could be cantilevered 10 feet beyond the property line to gain footage.

In exchange, an equivalent amount of space could be devoted to retail space and other community uses, thus providing a perimeter of street-front commercial life without the loss of one square foot of convention space. The cantilever would have the additional benefit of protecting shoppers from the weather. A rejuvenated community and thousands of conventioneers would provide the market for this retail space.

With these two design changes in the design of the convention center, a behemoth of a building would become much more acceptable to many more Washingtonians.

—*Arthur Cotton Moore*
is a Washington architect.

Our idea was to respect the historic Carnegie Library by curving the front of the building. Also, we would inset the first floor on the North/South streets to add commercial uses to enliven them, and to protect pedestrians from inclement weather.

Washington Post (April 1997)

A NEW WAY FOR DOWNTOWN URBAN RENEWAL

Instead of complete demolition, as was done in our Southwest, the idea was to place columns in the backyards/alleys of the existing small-scale older buildings to support larger buildings. (This concept has been appropriated elsewhere by others who simply attached old facades directly to the new buildings—giving rise to the term "facadomy".)

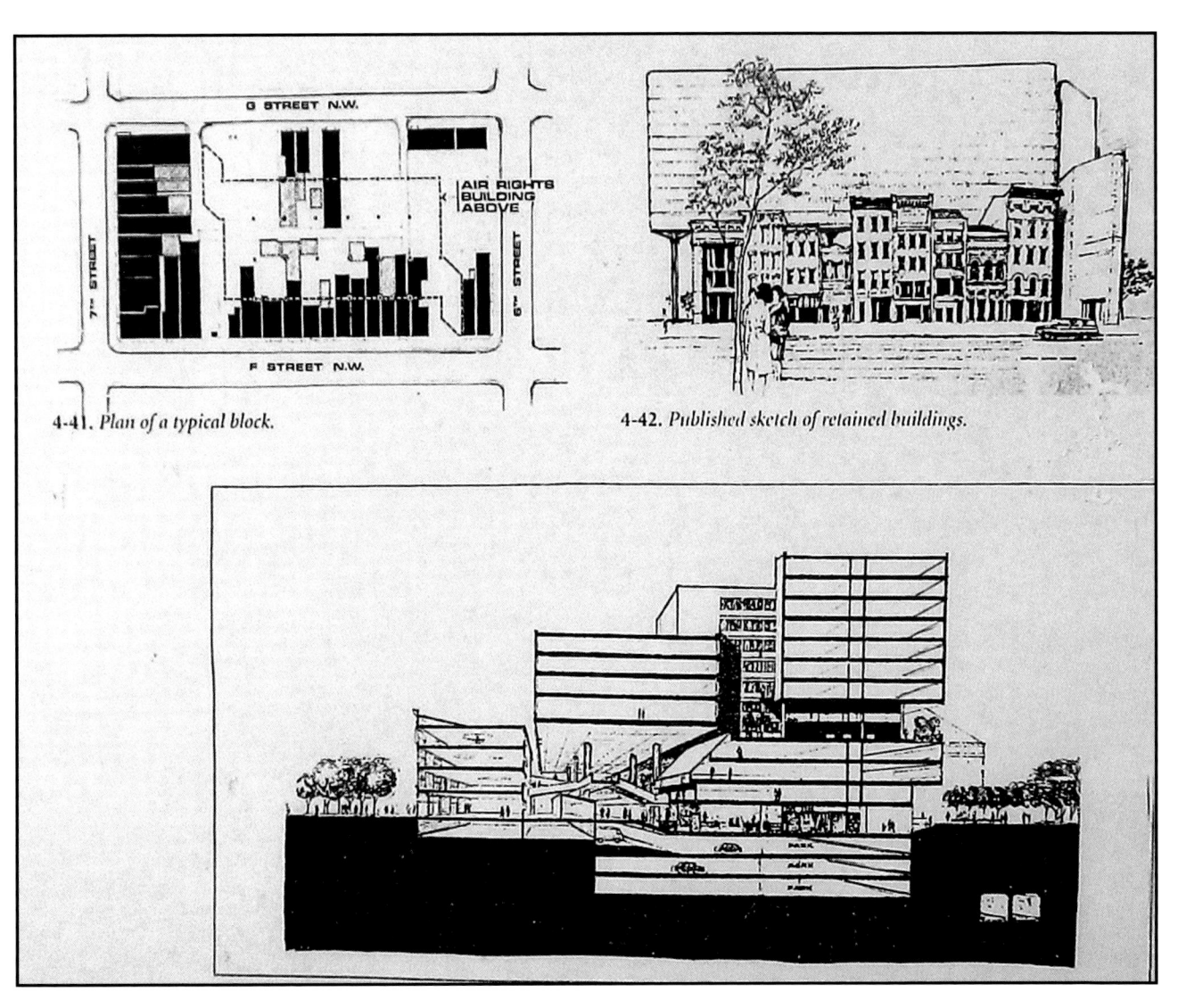

4-41. *Plan of a typical block.*

4-42. *Published sketch of retained buildings.*

Published in these newspapers in 1971 and 1972: *Washington Post* (25 stories) and *Evening Star* (14 stories). *DC Gazette* (October 1971); *Intowner* (November 1971); *Advocate* (November 1971); *Daily News* (November 1971); and *Frederick News* (June 1973).

Published in these magazines: *Progressive Architecture* (October 1971); *The American Institute of Architects Journal* (1974); and *Architectural Record* magazine (December 1977); and also in our book, *The Powers of Preservation*, published by McGraw-Hill (1998).

Stories were broadcast in these media: *NBC News* (October 1971, 7:00 a.m. and 11:00 p.m.); WMAL-TV (October 1971); and *CBS Morning Show* (October 1971).

POP-UP RETAIL AT THE TYSONS CORNER SILVER LINE

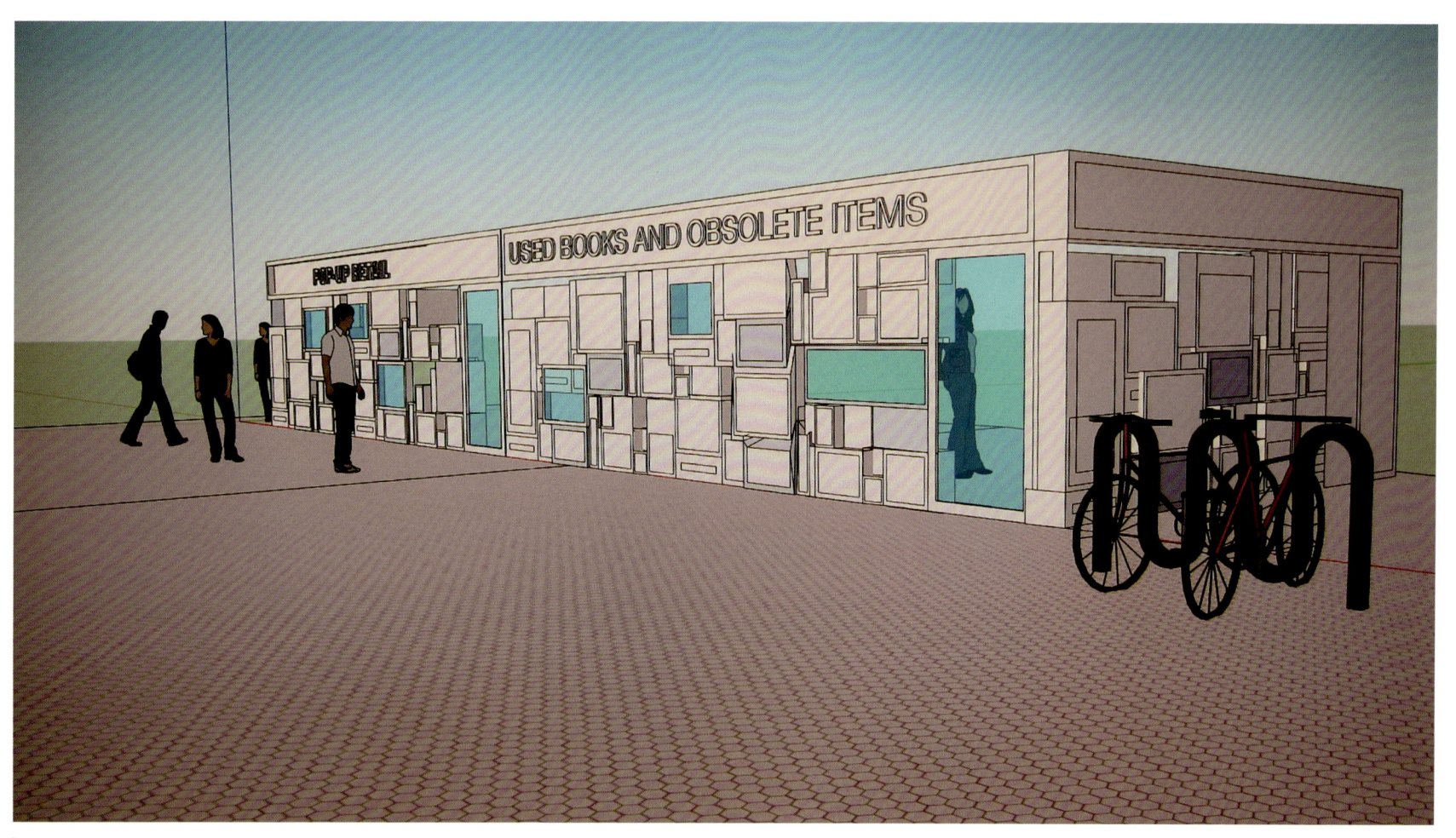

The Fairfax County government was looking for ideas for pop-up, temporary retail for Silver Line stations. Our scheme would be built out of the discarded detritus from the nearby abundance of office buildings, which largely include obsolete office machines.

THE WASHINGTON METROPOLITAN AREA

7 INVITATIONS TO CREATE CONCEPT DESIGNS

A ROOF FOR THE CARTER BARRON AMPHITHEATRE

The Carter Barron, located in Rock Creek Park, has always been hampered by being an open-air space. In 1997, the Friends of Carter Barron asked us to design a way to protect performances from rain during the summer.

A summer roof comprising inflatable elements held in place by cables would protect performers and the audience from rain and would make Carter Barron a fully operational facility. Unfortunately, its Friends were unable to raise the necessary funds.

DETAIL: helium filled lily pad shaped inflatables, interlocking valleys, drain line, main cable, gas valve

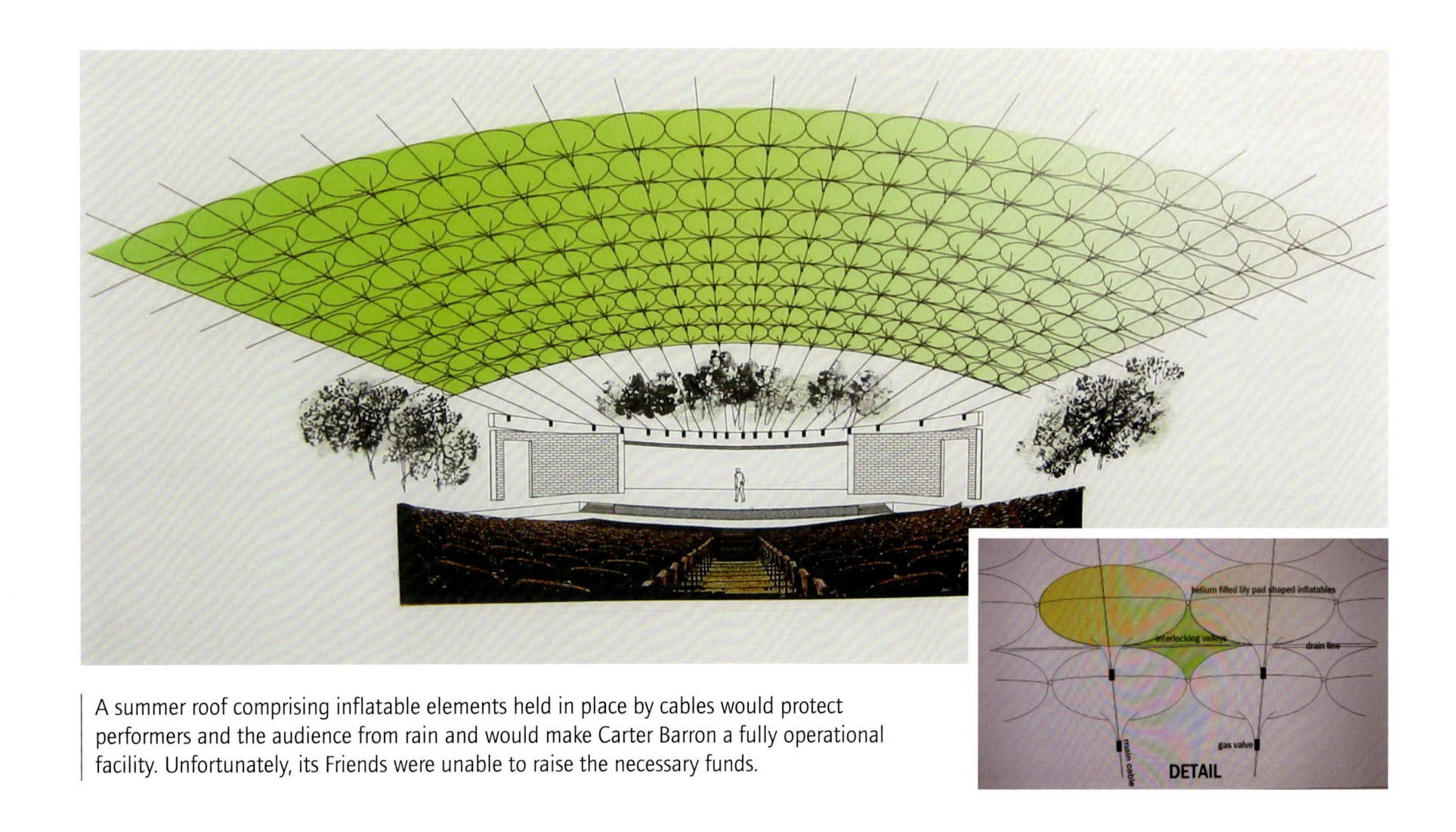

INVITATIONS TO CREATE CONCEPT DESIGNS

ANACOSTIA PERFORMING ARTS CENTER

The late, former mayor, then-council member Marion Barry, asked us to do a design concept on the East Campus of St. Elizabeths.

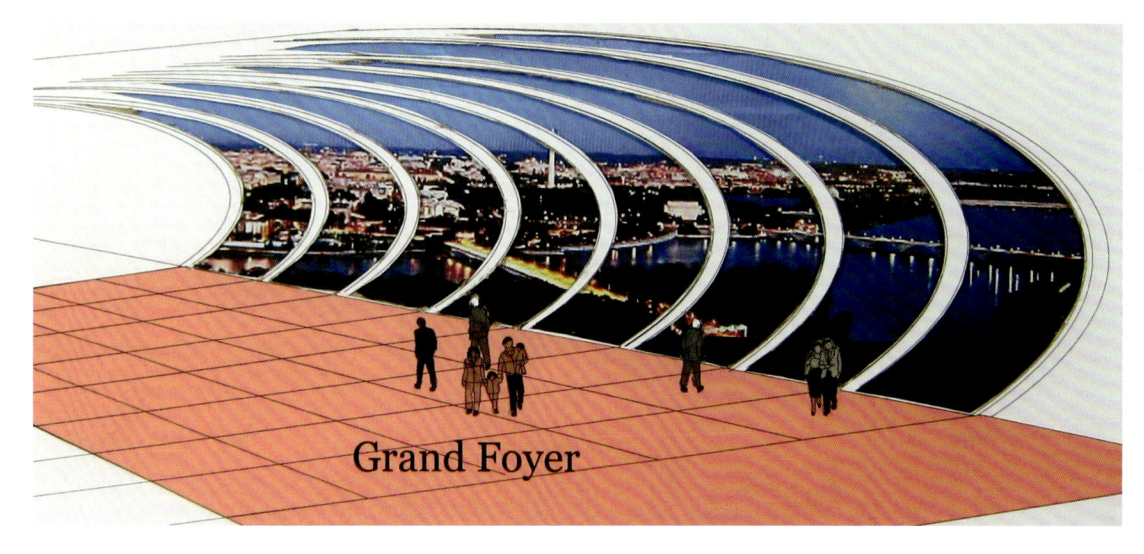

A conceptual design of the Grand Foyer. (The shown view of the city is for illustrative purposes only.)

PLAN OF ANACOSTIA PERFORMING ARTS CENTER

- parking
- parking
- panoramic view of the city
- FOYER
- performance
- dance | support | M
- performance
- dance | support | W
- Admin
- tickets
- route from Congress Heights Metro Station
- parking
- parking

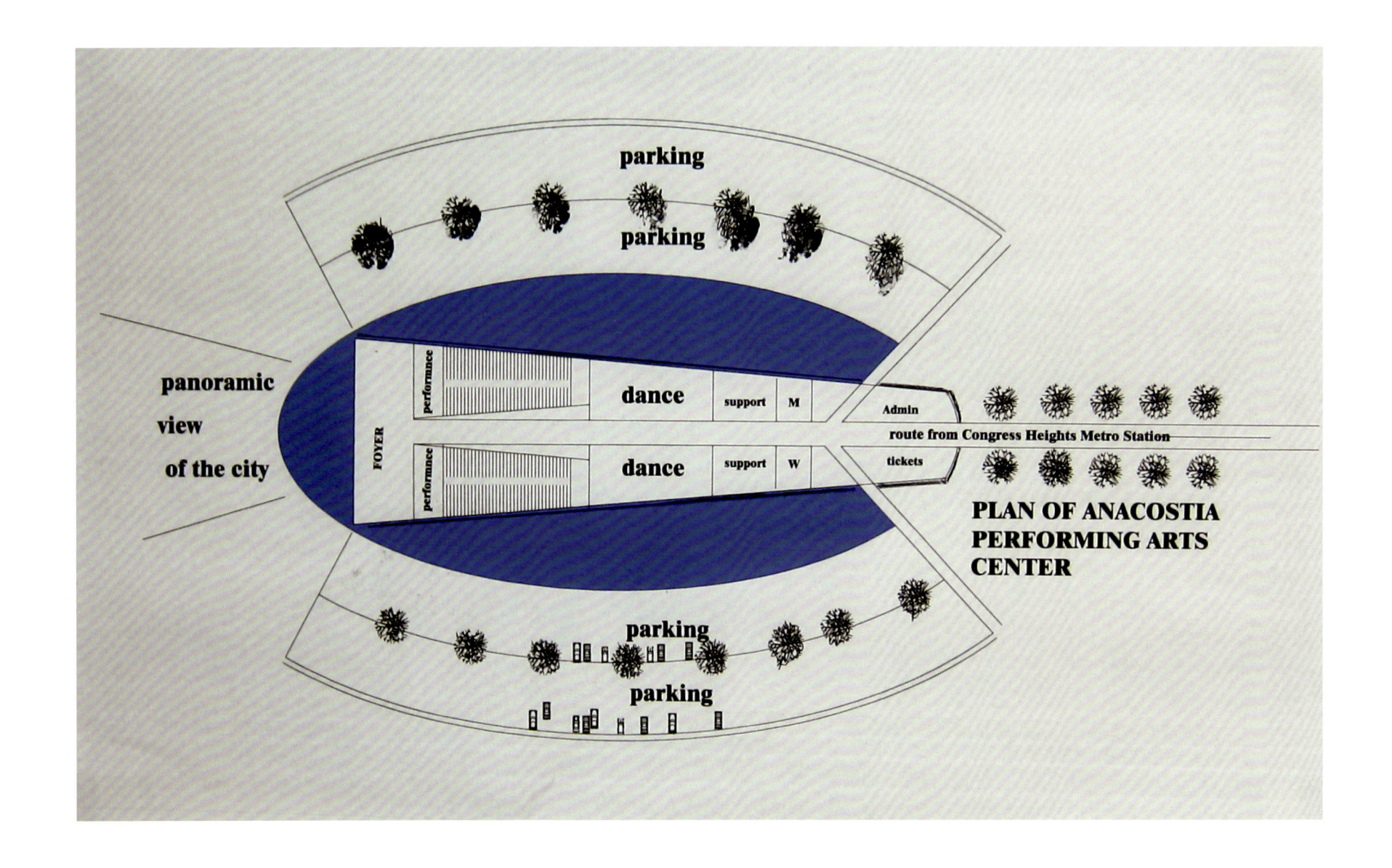

INVITATIONS TO CREATE CONCEPT DESIGNS

A PATENT MUSEUM AT THE COMMERCE DEPARTMENT

Secretary Baldridge asked for our help with his proposed Inventors and Entrepreneurs Museum. After his death, the museum was moved to Virginia. The interior is now used as a museum for the White House.

FORT LINCOLN: A NEW TOWN IN TOWN

Wolf von Eckardt, then-architecture critic of the *Washington Post*, asked us to visualize the new town of Fort Lincoln, which had been proposed by President Johnson. (Our original image was published, and then lost; this sketch is a re-creation.) The inclusion of a heliport is no longer possible after 9/11.

INVITATIONS TO CREATE CONCEPT DESIGNS

NEW USES FOR ST. ELIZABETHS WEST CAMPUS

The late Ambassador Mark Palmer asked us to develop a concept to reuse the (then empty) historic buildings. The yellow canopies link those buildings together, which would predominately comprise an Art Village.

Proposed Firehouse Café at St. Elizabeths Art Village, from our 1999 Master Plan.

8 FEDERAL GOVERNMENT BUILDINGS

THE FBI BUILDING'S BLANK WALL ON PENNSYLVANIA AVENUE (1998)

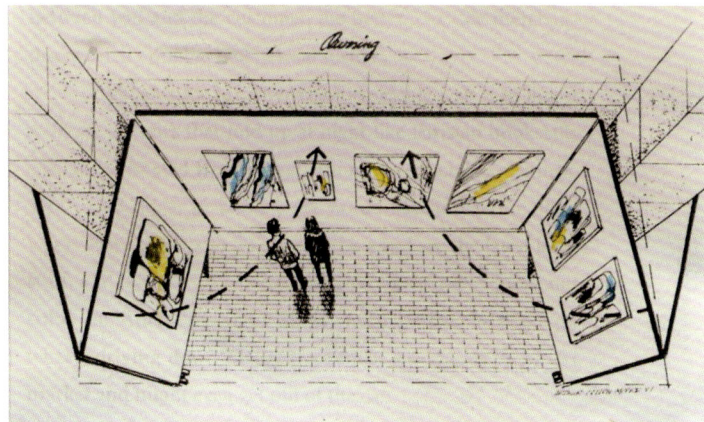

Our idea was to install a "Temporary Contemporary" along the wall to bring some life and activity to this desolate block along America's Main Street.

KEEPING THE FBI IN WASHINGTON ON FALLOW FEDERAL LAND (2013)

The General Services Administration is planning to remove the FBI from its building on Pennsylvania Avenue. We believe that the agency must remain in the District, in convenient proximity to Congress and the Federal Government. Our scheme shows that the FBI Headquarters could be accommodated on the empty lot behind the Government Printing Office, which is near a Metro station, Union Station, and a Circulator stop.

Washingtonian magazine (April 2013)

THE JOHN ADAMS MEMORIAL IN THE JOHN ADAMS BUILDING. THE LIBRARY OF CONGRESS

The Memorial at the south entrance. Statues are of Abigail, John, and John Quincy Adams.

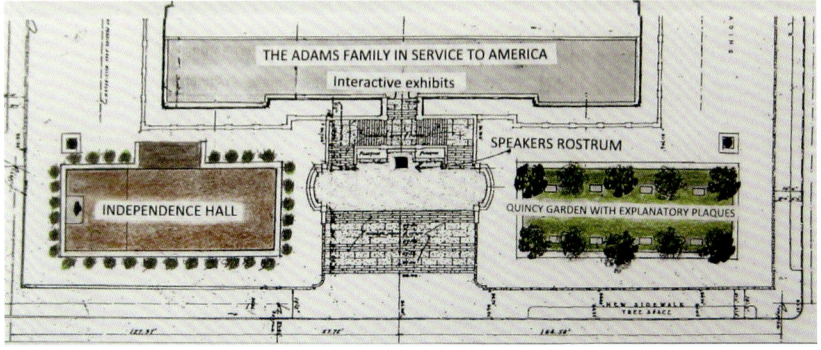

Plan showing interior and exterior.

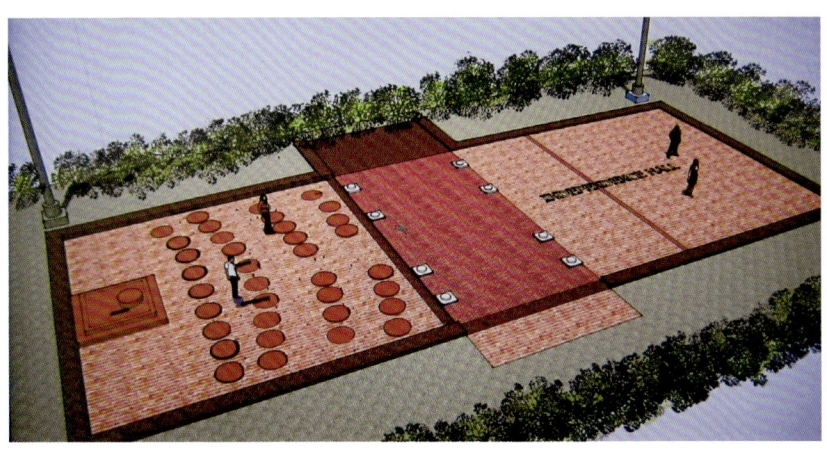

The symbolic landscape design of Philadelphia's Independence Hall would be done in paving materials to reflect the location of some of John Adams' finest hours.

9 THE NATIONAL MALL AND THE MONUMENTAL CORE

HAPPY 100th BIRTHDAY OF THE NATIONAL PARK SERVICE

Our idea had tethered hot-air balloons floating above L'Enfant's cross-axis, so people could see the overall concept of the L'Enfant and McMillan Plans, delineated by solar light fixtures.

AMENITY FOR VISITORS TO THE WASHINGTON MONUMENT GROUNDS

Tourists must cross the extensive Washington Monument grounds to get to the other side of the Mall. Given our brutal summer heat, we thought they deserve to rest their hot, tired feet in a tree-shaded artificial stream that runs across the southern boundary of the Monument's grounds. We sited this path so they are able to see the North/South axis, with views north to the White House and south to the Jefferson Memorial.

We discovered this terrific feature in Chicago's Millennium Park. If our National Park Service would like to do it here, we are confident that a license from the copyright holder and a plaque acknowledging Millennium Park could be accomplished.

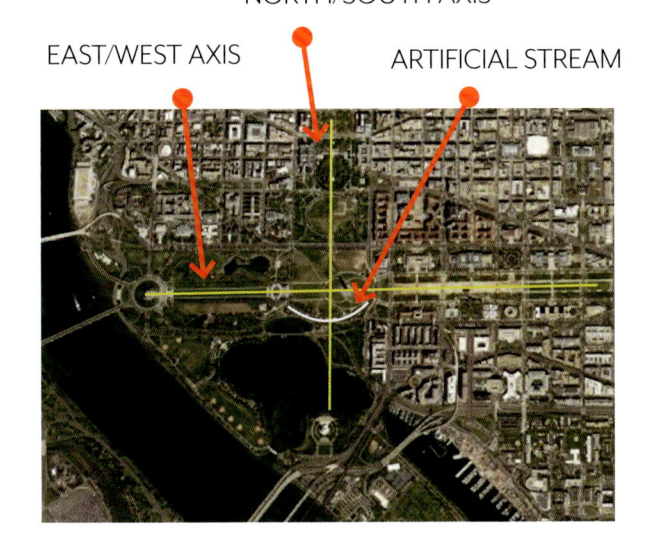

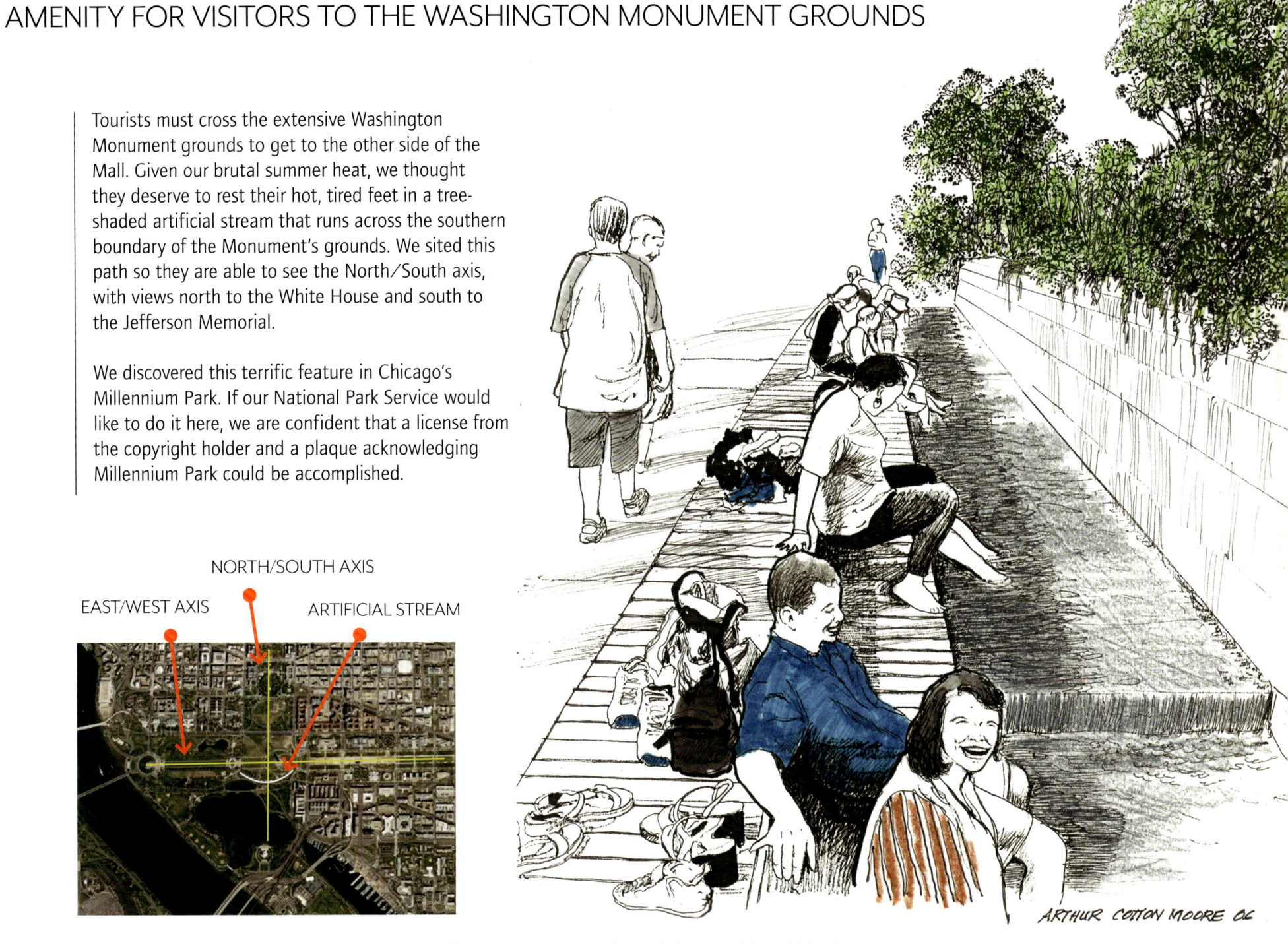

Our Nation's Capital: *Pro Bono Publico* Ideas | proffered by ARTHUR COTTON MOORE FAIA ©

ALTERNATIVE SITES FOR FESTIVALS REMOVED FROM THE MALL

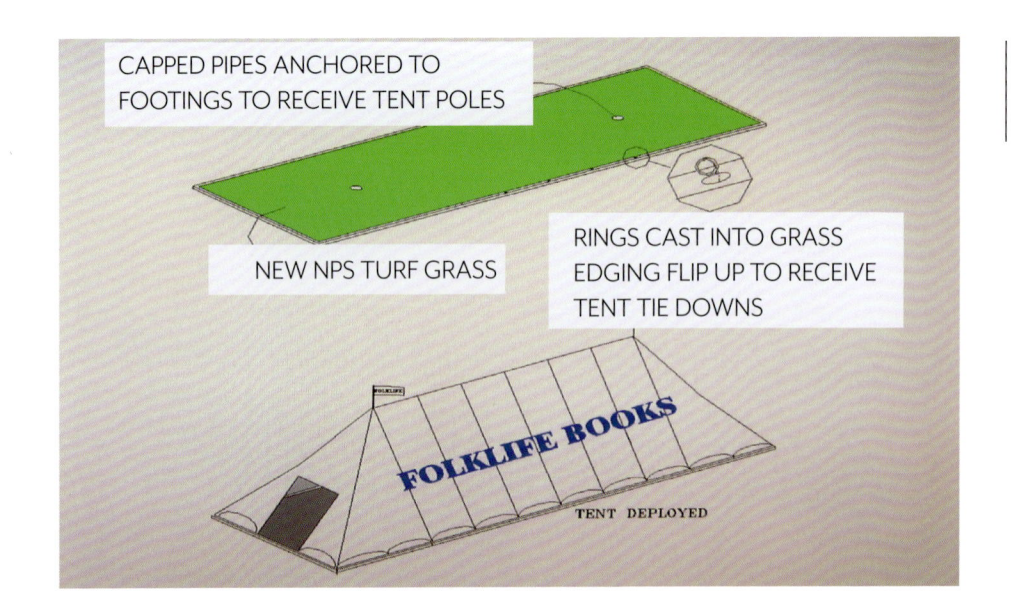

Alternative A keeps the festivals on the Mall, without harming the new irrigation system for the grass panels.

Alternative B relocates the Folklife Festival to 10th Street (L'Enfant Promenade).

THE NATIONAL MALL AND THE MONUMENTAL CORE

LINKING THE MALL VIA MEMORIAL BRIDGES

Our idea creates new memorial sites on the Mall by linking it together with memorials that incorporate functioning bridges, forming a continuous safe pedestrian experience from the Capitol to the Lincoln Memorial.

MEMORIAL STATUES WITH EXPLANATORY PLAQUES.
EXAMPLE: THE CHARLES BRIDGE IN PRAGUE.

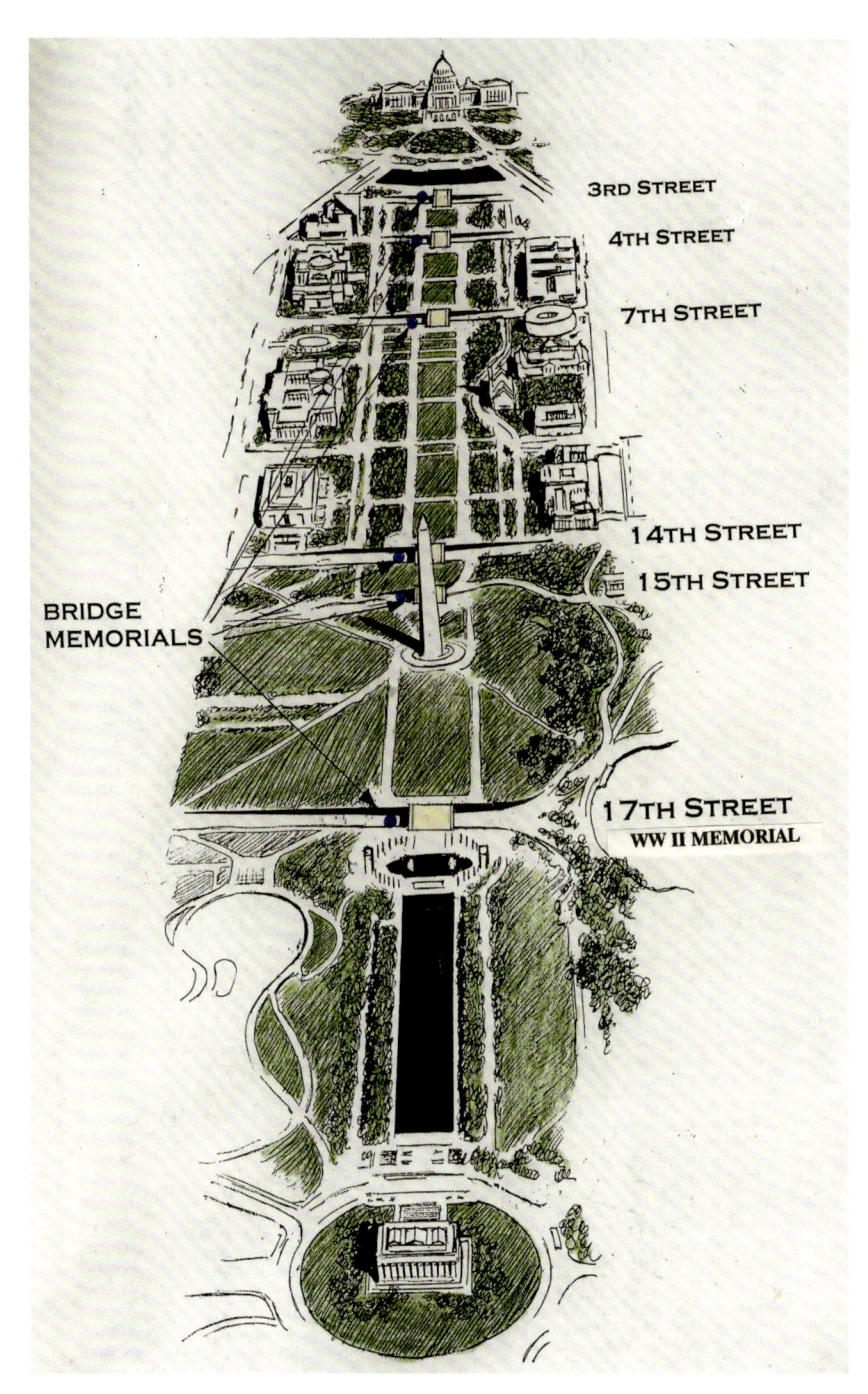

BRIDGE MEMORIALS

3RD STREET
4TH STREET
7TH STREET
14TH STREET
15TH STREET
17TH STREET
WW II MEMORIAL

LARGER CENTRAL STATUE

MEMORIAL BRIDGE ALTERNATIVES

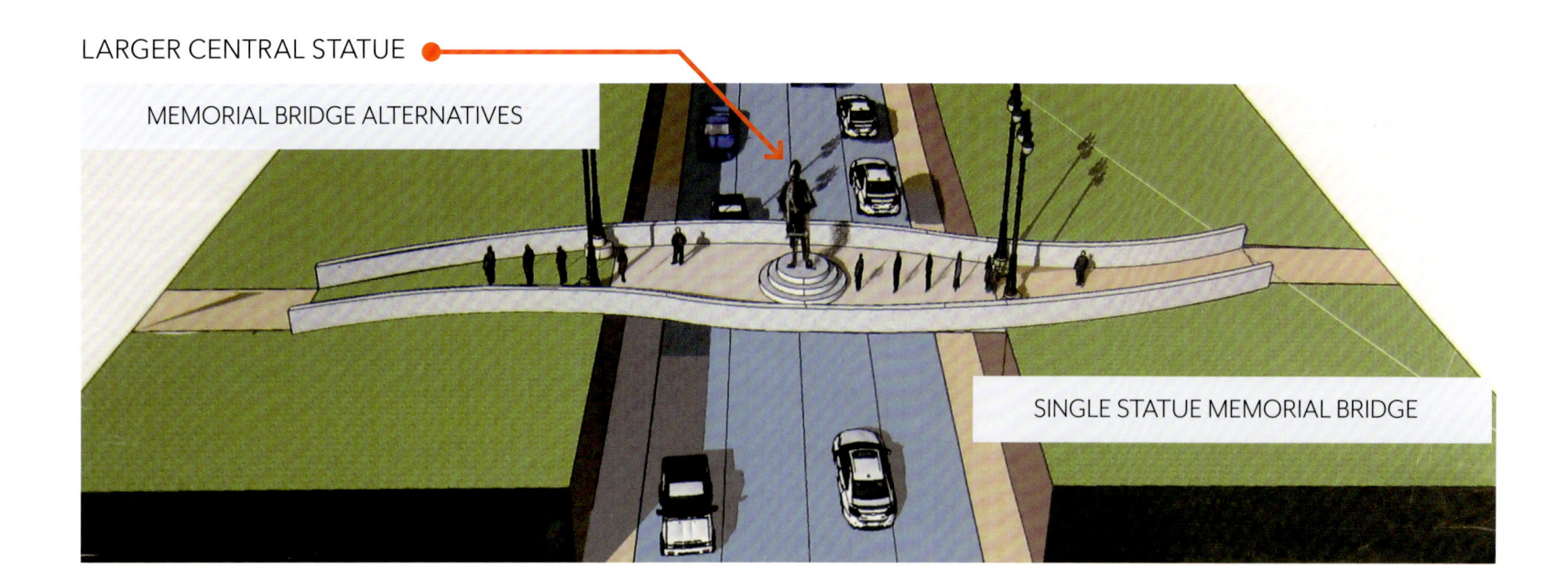

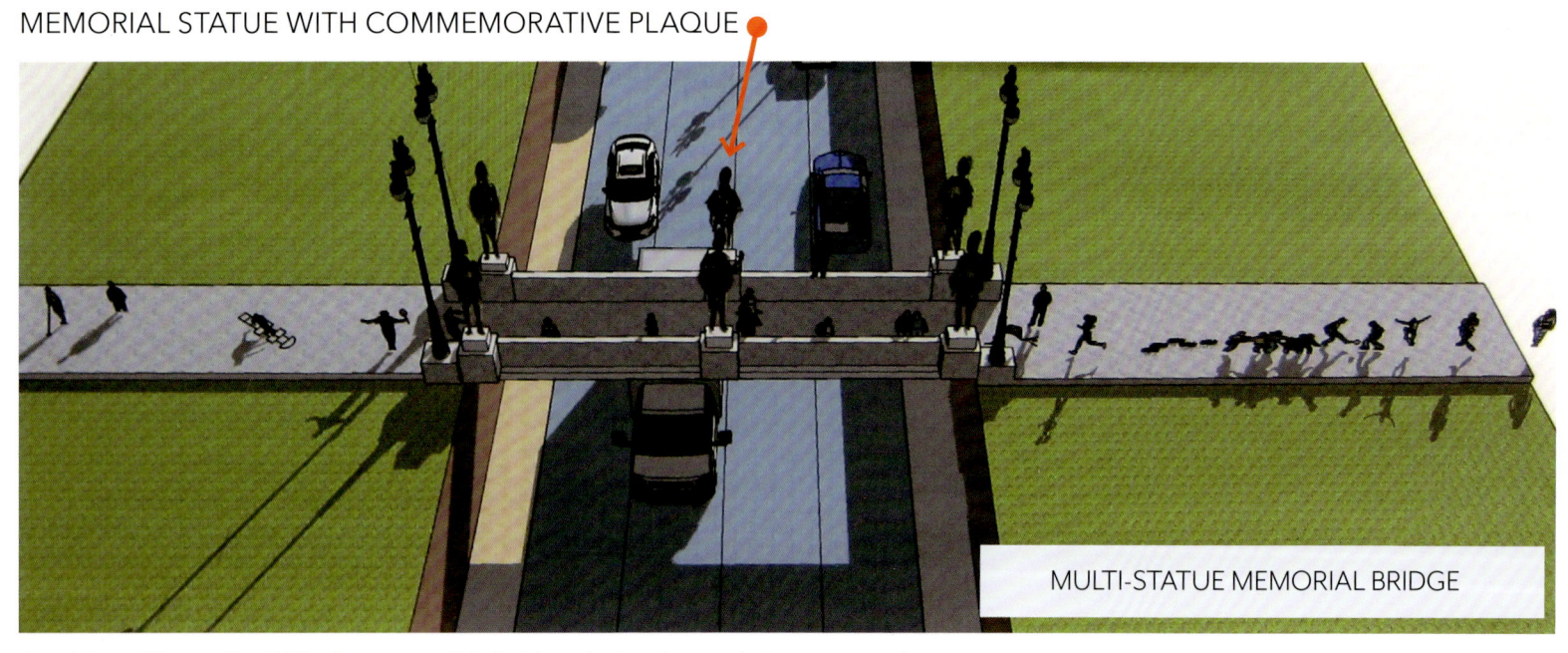

SINGLE STATUE MEMORIAL BRIDGE

MEMORIAL STATUE WITH COMMEMORATIVE PLAQUE

MULTI-STATUE MEMORIAL BRIDGE

Our idea offers a flexibility to memorial/bridge design beyond these examples.

THE NATIONAL MALL AND THE MONUMENTAL CORE

WWII MEMORIAL WITH MAP BRIDGE

An example of a memorial bridge that would cross 17th Street. In this case, the bridge enhances and helps explain the WWII Memorial.

17th STREET LEVEE, LINKING THE WASHINGTON MONUMENT GROUNDS TO THE LINCOLN MEMORIAL AREA

Existing stalled levee since the beginning of 2014.

Integral to the finished levee design is a labor-and-time intensive stop-log flood control system across 17th Street. This installation is to keep Potomac River flood waters from inundating downtown.

THE NATIONAL MALL AND THE MONUMENTAL CORE

The levee was completed in 2015, but not at the height recommended by the Army Corps of Engineers.

Our idea is to use the existing levee walls, and to raise them modestly—to the Corps' standards—to support a bridge spanning heavily trafficked 17th Street. That will provide safe pedestrian and bicycle movement between the Washington Monument grounds and the Lincoln Memorial grounds.

17th Street Levee Supporting Pedestrian Bridge

ARTHUR COTTON MOORE/ASSOCIATES
ARCHITECTS   PLANNERS
WASHINGTON D.C.   COPYRIGHT 2015

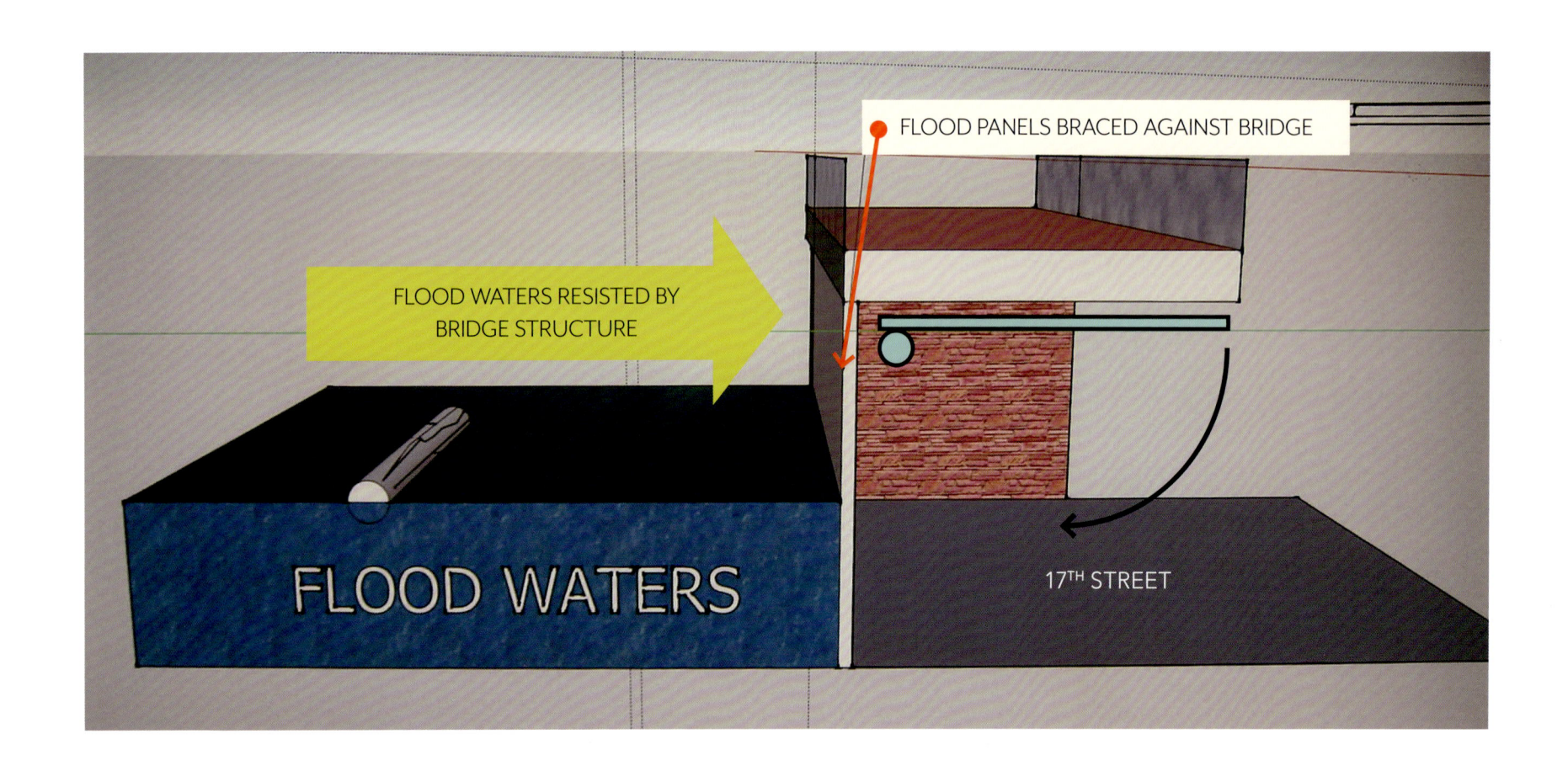

Diagram of deployed swing-down flood panels located on the underside of the bridge to form a floodgate wall. This floodgate system would be rapidly deployable, stronger, and at a higher elevation than the proposed stop-log system.

THE NATIONAL MALL AND THE MONUMENTAL CORE

ENHANCING THE SCOPE OF THE DISTRICT OF COLUMBIA WAR MEMORIAL

A world map would make it a memorial for all U.S. WWI veterans.

L'ENFANT FESTIVAL PROMENADE: LINKING THE MALL TO THE SOUTHWEST WATERFRONT

This long and barren bridge-walk is one direct link over the Southwest Freeway to the southwest portion of the city and its waterfront.

WALK OVER SOUTHWEST FREEWAY | SOUTHWEST FREEWAY

FORRESTAL BUILDING—PART OF THE ENERGY DEPARTMENT

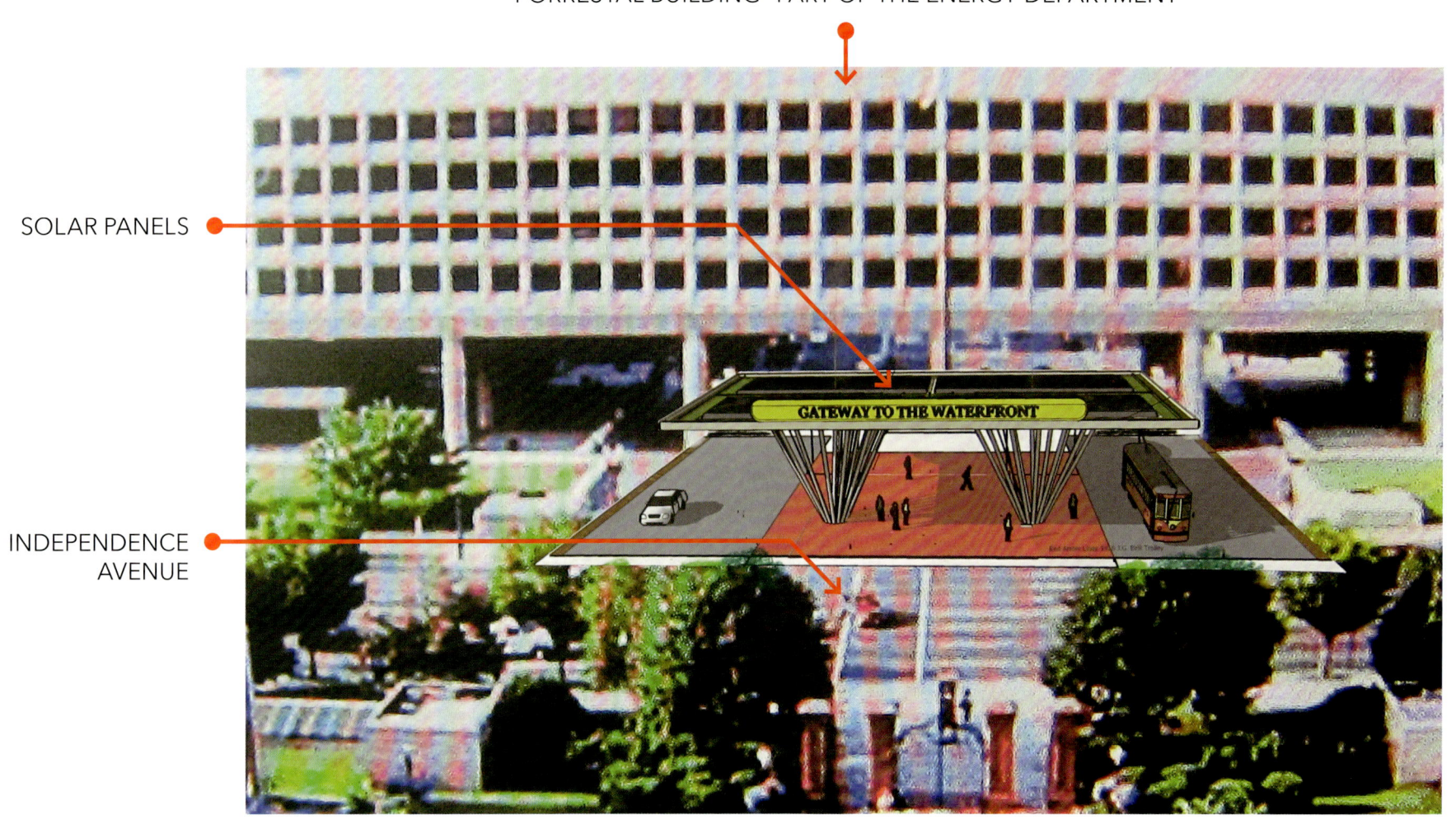

SOLAR PANELS

GATEWAY TO THE WATERFRONT

INDEPENDENCE AVENUE

View from the Smithsonian Castle to the entrance of the L'Enfant Festival Promenade, which uses 10th Street as a link down to the Southwest Waterfront.

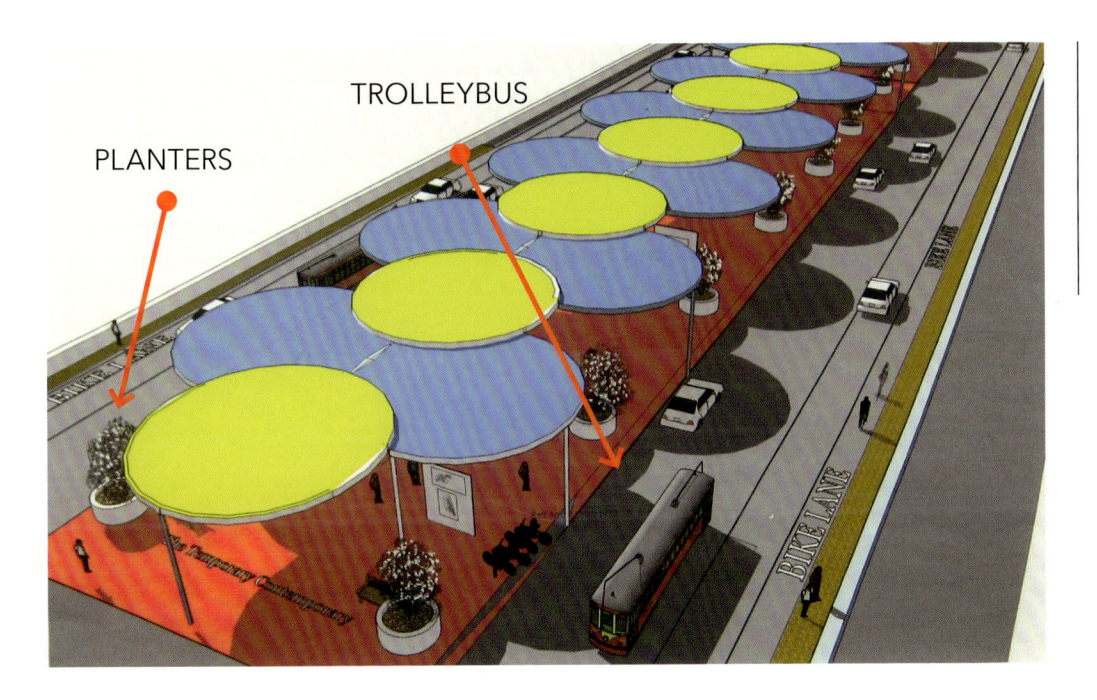

PLANTERS TROLLEYBUS

Our idea is overlapping canopies—to provide continuous protection from sun and rain—that are anchored from the wind by ties to planters. The Promenade is easily taken down for winter, and provides space for all manner of markets and festivals.

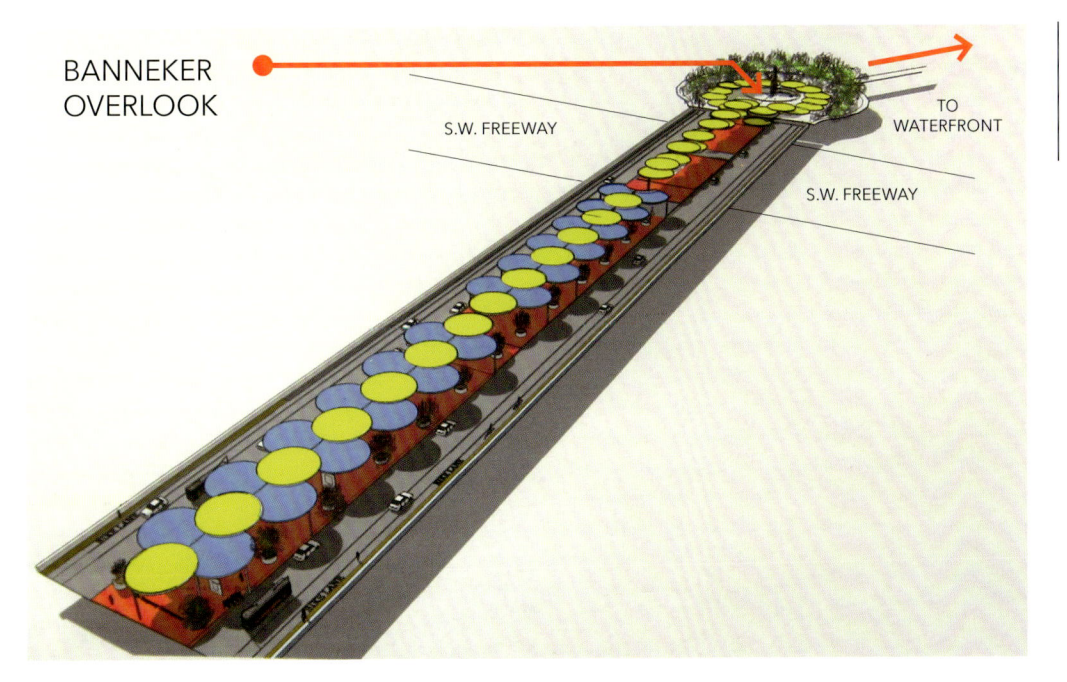

BANNEKER OVERLOOK S.W. FREEWAY TO WATERFRONT S.W. FREEWAY

Linked canopies provide weather-protected access to Banneker Overlook and the Southwest Waterfront.

Our Nation's Capital: *Pro Bono Publico* Ideas | proffered by ARTHUR COTTON MOORE FAIA ©

The covered area would be available for summer festivals, art shows, farmers' markets, and such.

10 AN ARCHITECTURAL MODEL OF OUR NATION'S CAPITAL

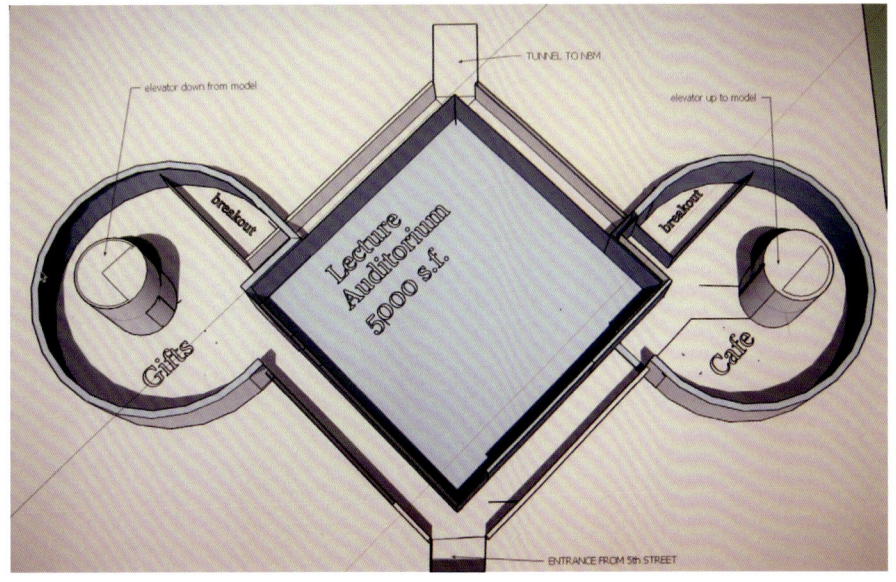

A PAVILION ON THE VACANT LAND ADJACENT TO THE NATIONAL BUILDING MUSEUM

The model would be an educational tool for students. It would be useful to the National Capital Planning Commission, the Commission of Fine Arts, the Historic Preservation Review Board, and all other reviewing and regulatory agencies within the D.C. and Federal Government, as well as civic organizations. The model would also become a major tourist attraction, benefited by a Metro stop across the street.

GROUND FLOOR FACILITIES

On the first level, the Pavilion would house a lecture auditorium, a café, gift shop, and break-out spaces; the second level would house the model, viewing sites, and robotic cars with cameras. The levels would be connected by stairs and elevators.

Our Nation's Capital: *Pro Bono Publico* Ideas | proffered by ARTHUR COTTON MOORE FAIA ©

5 TH STREET

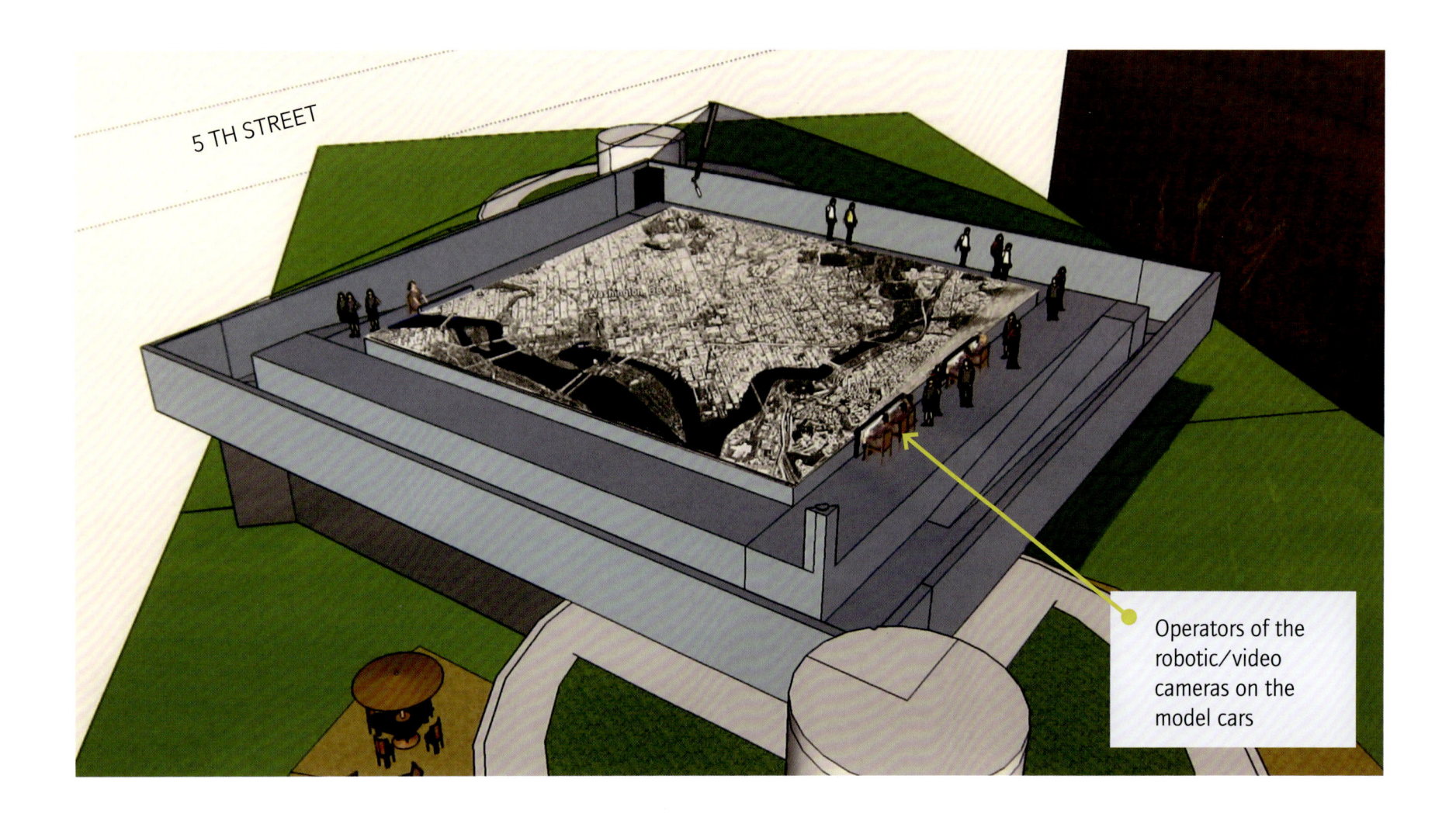

Operators of the robotic/video cameras on the model cars

Our model reflects the diamond shape of Washington. At 60 feet, and scaled at 1 inch equals 40 feet, it represents 5.45 miles on each side.

AN ARCHITECTURAL MODEL OF OUR NATION'S CAPITAL

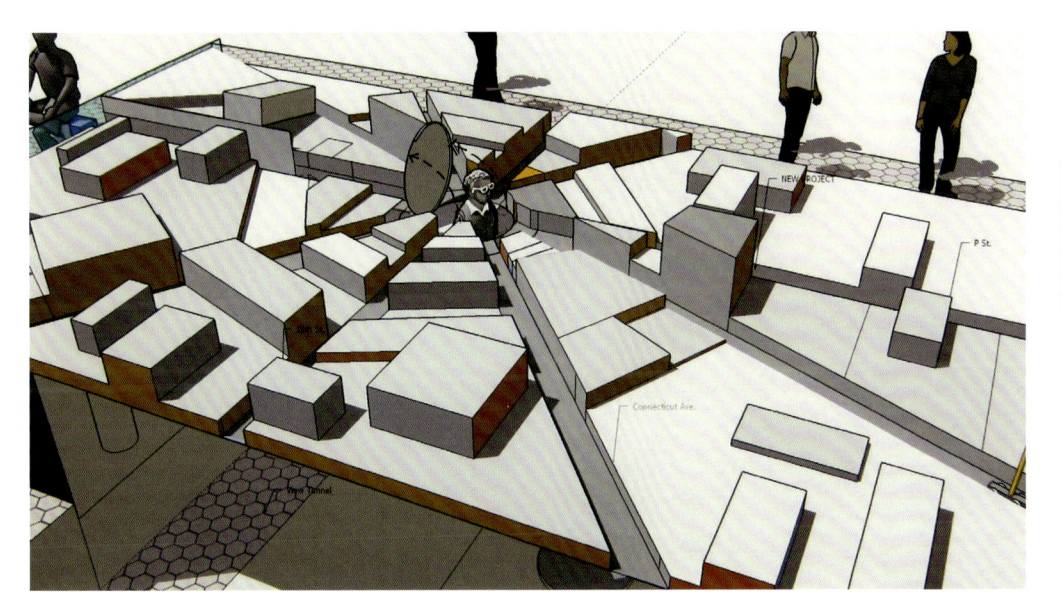

UPPER LEVEL OF MODEL

Allows placement of proposed new structures, removal of demolished structures, proposed urban design elements, and such.

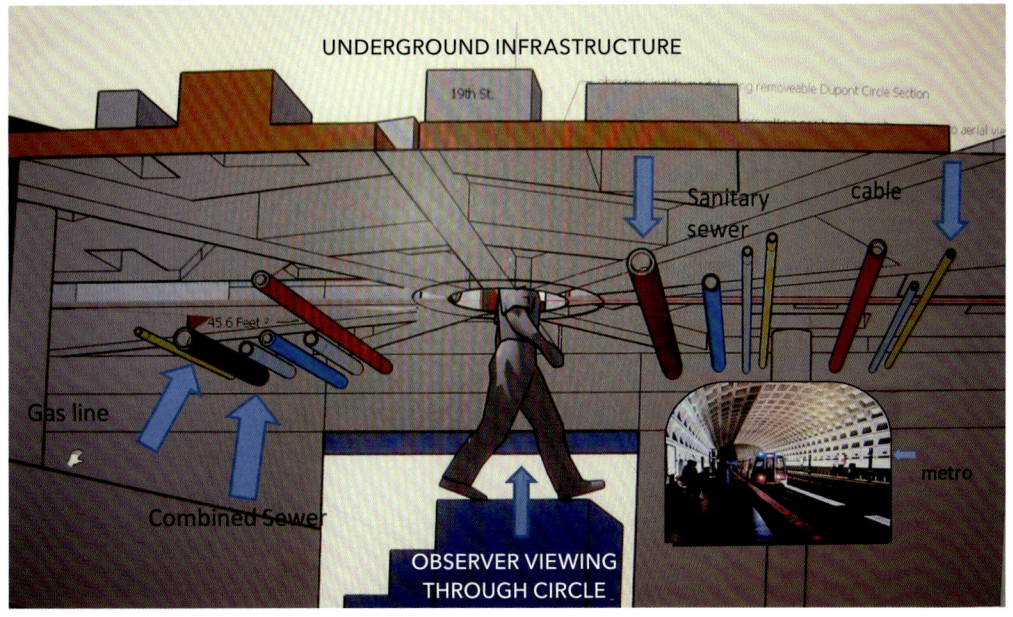

LOWER LEVEL OF MODEL

Could include utility lines and Metro, seen from passages under the model.

REMOTE CONTROL CAMERA-CARS AROUND DUPONT CIRCLE

Robotic cars fitted with adjustable video cameras move along the model's streets, providing multiple views of changes in the city. These camera-cars will be driven by operators watching monitors on the perimeter of the model.

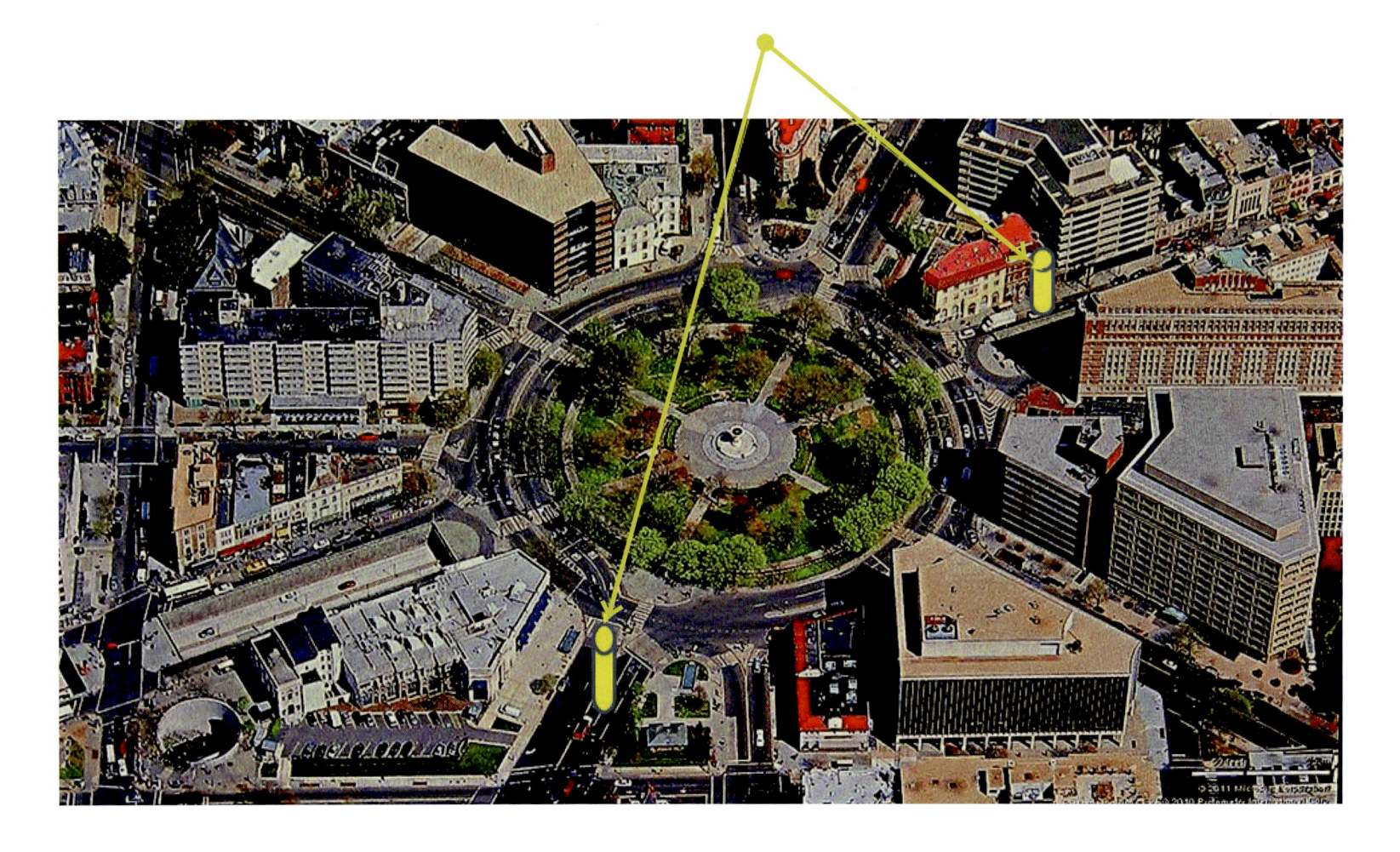

AN ARCHITECTURAL MODEL OF OUR NATION'S CAPITAL

AERIAL VIEW OF THE PAVILION

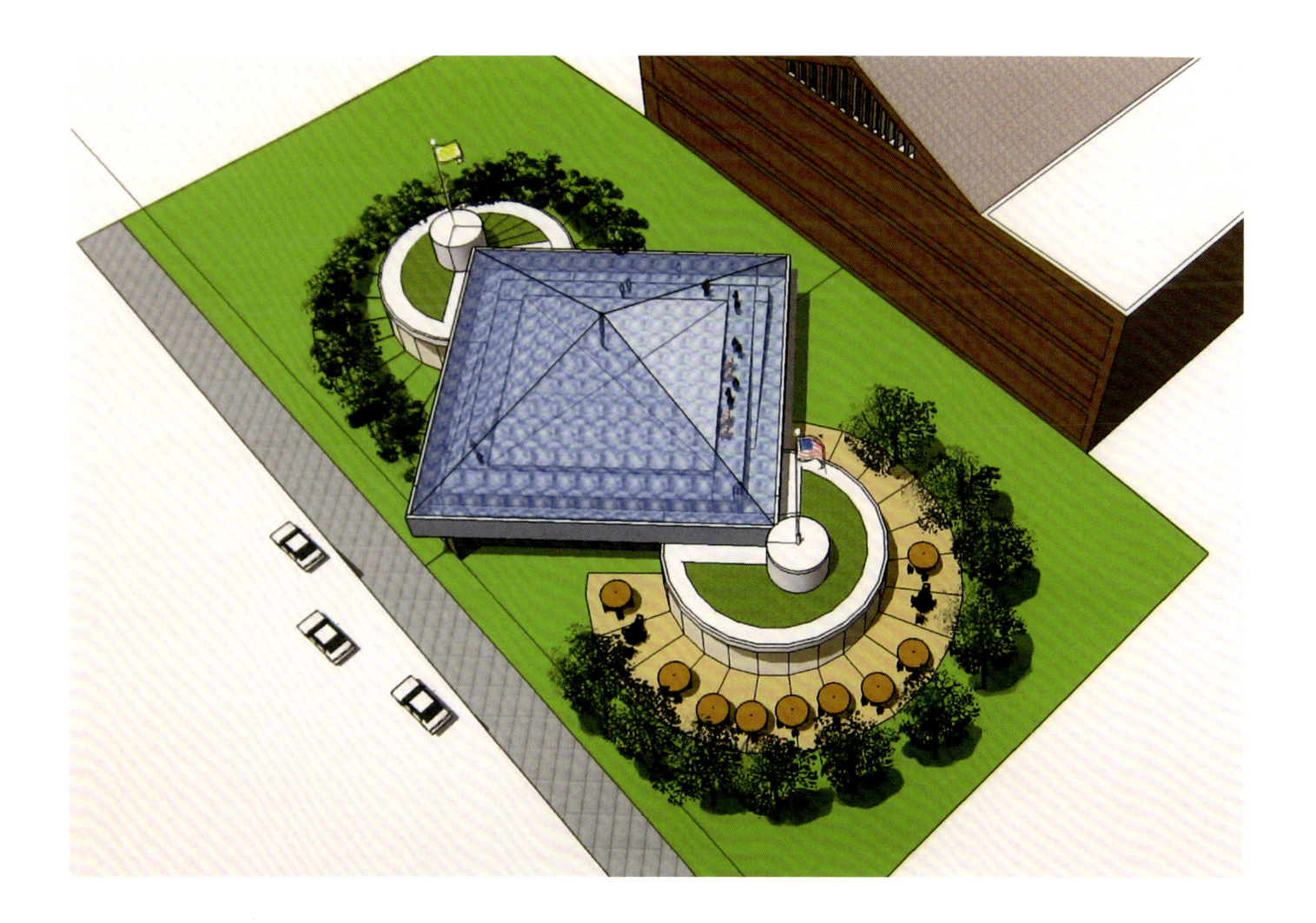

The Pavilion would have an underground connection to the National Building Museum.

11 THE NATIONAL MALL UNDERGROUND

The multi-use National Mall Underground project carries forward the conclusion of the 2011 study undertaken by D.C. and Federal Government agencies in response to the internal (not from the river) storm-water flood of 2006, which damaged many Federal and Smithsonian buildings. It has these benefits:

- At flood times around Constitution Avenue (where Tiber Creek used to be) it will act as a reservoir, taking in flood waters.

- It will contain cisterns, which will catch rainwater and ground water from the nearby buildings for irrigation of the entire Mall, which is now partially irrigated by the National Park Service purchasing expensive treated potable water.

- It will ameliorate air pollution by providing below-grade tour bus parking, in place of the present situation of lines of parked buses on city streets with their engines idling, which also contributes to the city's high rate of asthma.

- It will increase public safety by having a section devoted to the tour bus drivers where they can rest, eat, and shower before continuing their travels.

- Car parking will be provided only for visitors to the museums and memorials on the Mall, not for commuters. The facility will be price-controlled, and will not open until late in the morning.

- It will include a Visitor Center to provide information, first aid, security, food facilities and toilets.

- A field of geothermal wells will be below the lowest level, which will greatly help to cool and heat the surrounding buildings.

Washington Post. Editorial. (31 March 2013)
Washingtonian magazine (November 2013 and March 2015)

ACCESS TO AND EXITS FROM THE UNDERGROUND GARAGE FROM INDEPENDENCE AVENUE

GENERAL SERVICES ADMINISTRATION PHOTOGRAPH OF THE 2006 FLOOD

> It shows the Internal Revenue Service Building at Constitution Avenue and 10th Street NW.

OUR VIABLE RESPONSE TO FLOODING IN THIS LOCATION

Our rendering of the 2006 internal (non-Potomac River) flood shows the extent of the flood waters, and their significant damage to federal buildings.

THE NATIONAL MALL UNDERGROUND

FLOOD CONTROL, IRRIGATION, TOUR BUS/MUSEUM VISITOR PARKING, OVER A GEOTHERMAL FIELD

GEOTHERMAL FIELD

FLOOD WATER

The white dash line shows the extent of the underground facility.

87 | Our Nation's Capital: *Pro Bono Publico* Ideas | proffered by ARTHUR COTTON MOORE FAIA ©

TOUR BUS/MUSEUM VISITOR PARKING

A parking garage for tour buses and the cars of museum and memorial visitors. The parking would not be for commuters because it would open in the late morning and would be controlled by price.

HOLDING RESERVOIR FOR CONSTITUTION AVENUE FLOOD WATERS

Lower levels of garage become a reservoir for Constitution Avenue flood waters.

LOWER LEVEL GEOTHERMAL FIELD OF WELLS

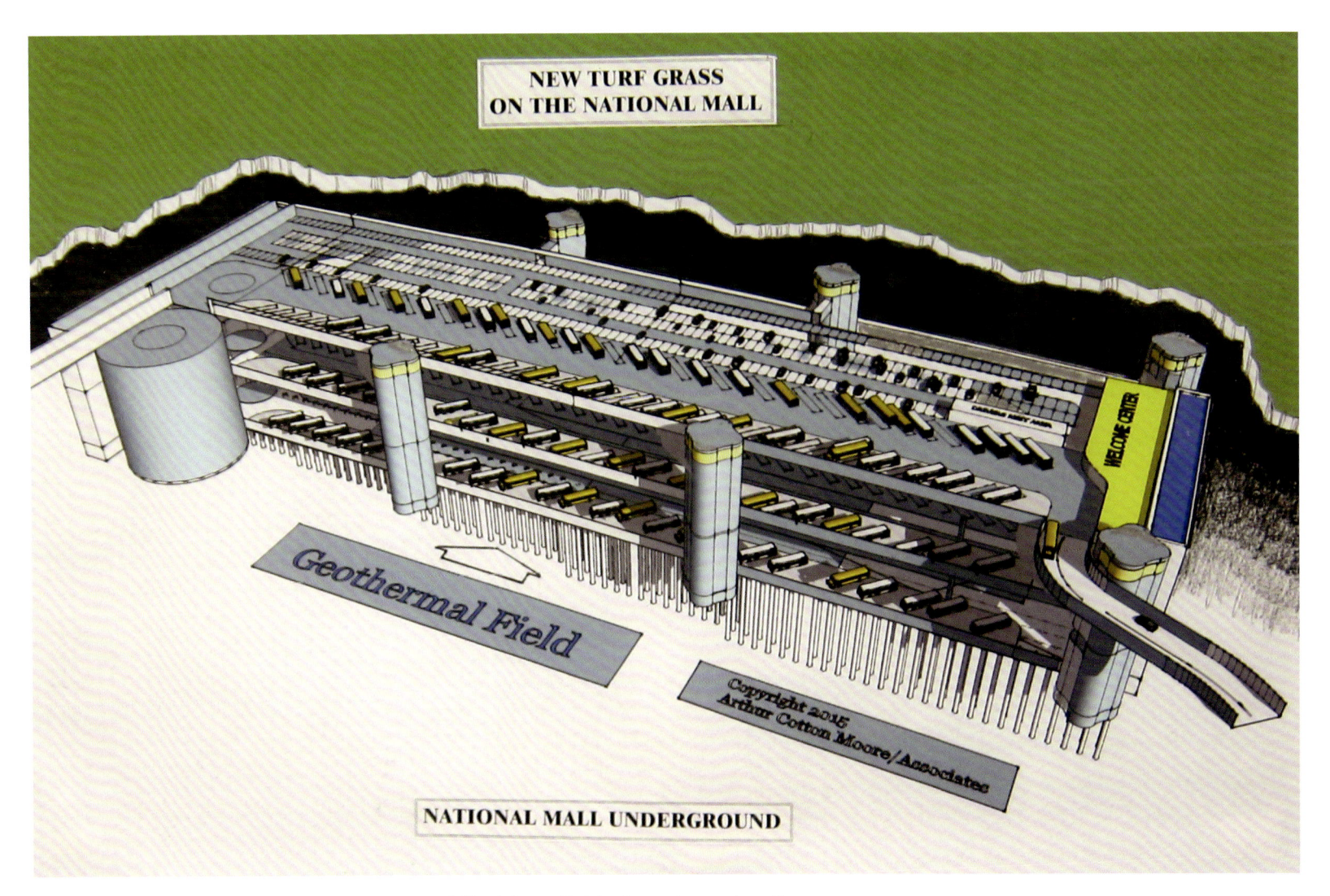

After excavation, the lower level would be drilled for a field of geothermal wells.

WASHINGTON HARBOUR FLOODING PROTOTYPE

Our Washington Harbour complex is a prototype for this project. The lower garage level at the Harbour is designed to be flooded at the river's high surge level, making it an operative example of how flood waters could be taken in by the National Mall Underground.

Lights on top of the flood pylons during a popular night.

Floodgates up for 2010 flood. Benches at far left have intakes to flood the lower level garage.

INTAKE UNDER CONCRETE BENCHES

FLOODGATES WERE PULLED UP APPROXIMATELY 60 TIMES BETWEEN 1986 AND 2016

THE NATIONAL MALL UNDERGROUND

CONCRETE BENCHES

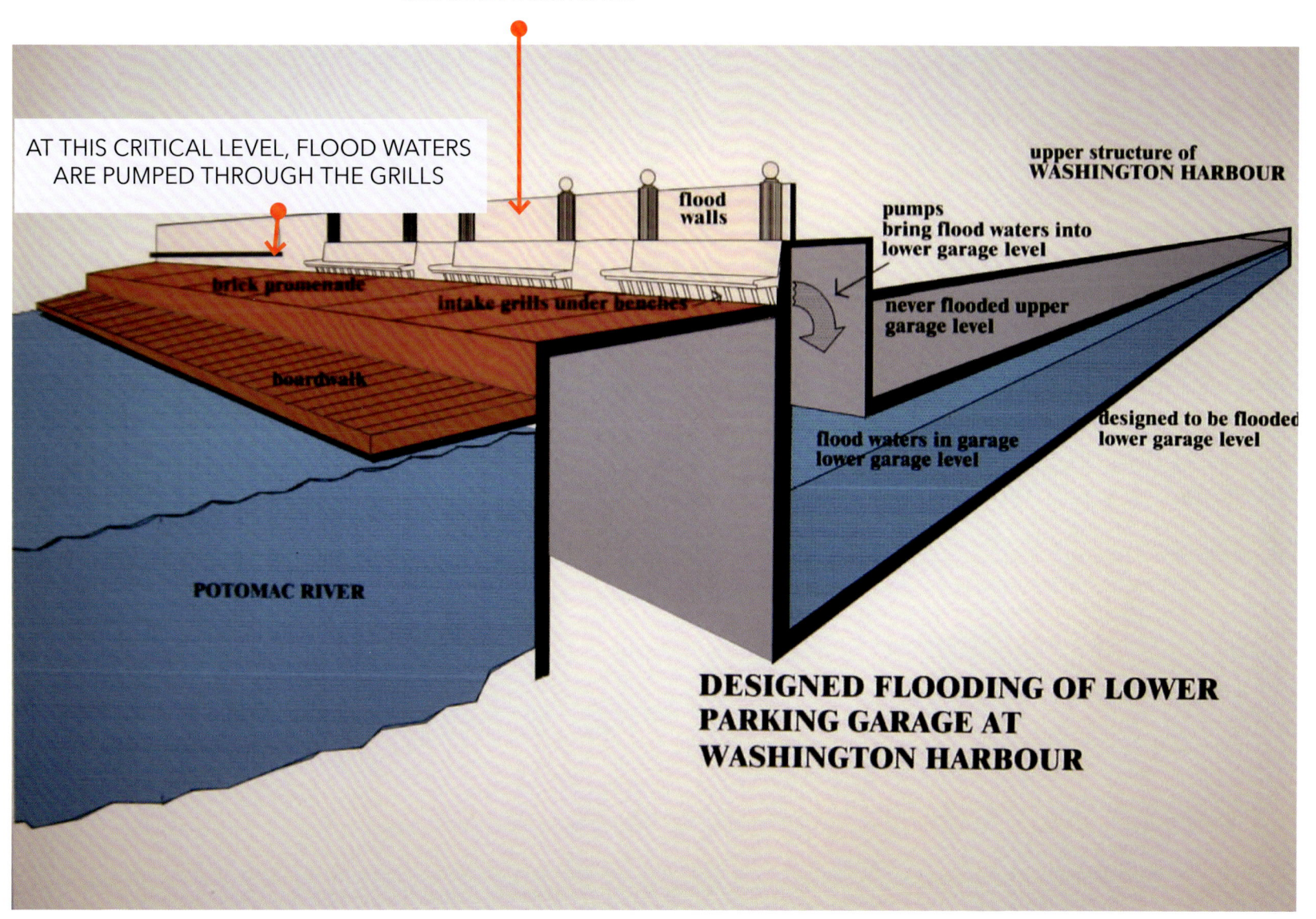

AT THIS CRITICAL LEVEL, FLOOD WATERS ARE PUMPED THROUGH THE GRILLS

upper structure of **WASHINGTON HARBOUR**

flood walls

pumps bring flood waters into lower garage level

brick promenade

intake grills under benches

never flooded upper garage level

boardwalk

flood waters in garage lower garage level

designed to be flooded lower garage level

POTOMAC RIVER

DESIGNED FLOODING OF LOWER PARKING GARAGE AT WASHINGTON HARBOUR

METHOD OF DETOXIFYING FLOOD WATERS
FROM CONSTITUTION AVENUE

A series of stepped wetlands with special grasses and microorganisms to purify water.

THE NATIONAL MALL UNDERGROUND

VISITOR CENTER/IRRIGATION CISTERN

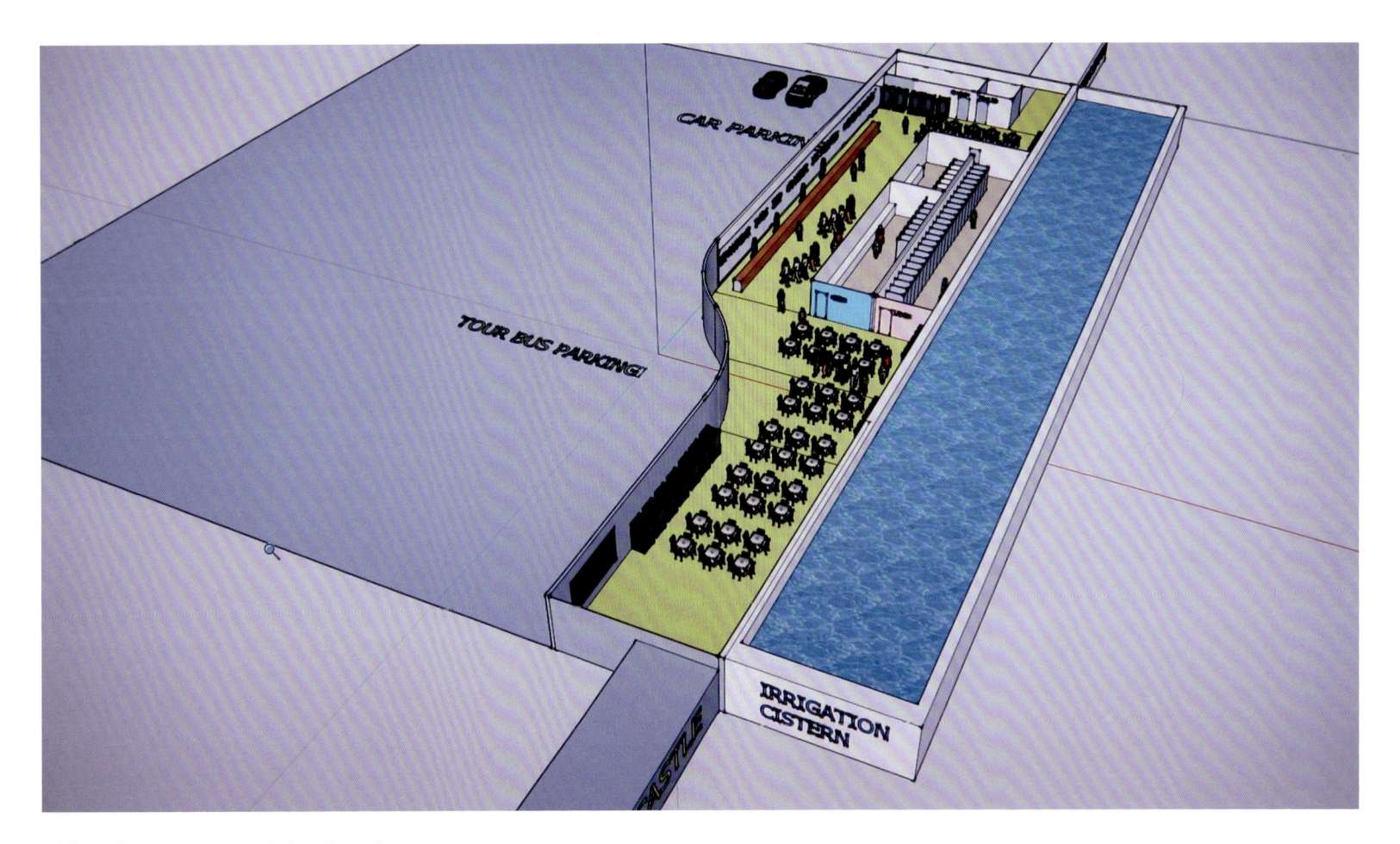

Visitor Center next to irrigation cistern.

ENTRANCE PAVILIONS

LED LIGHTS IN WALLS

GLASS STRUCTURAL WALL ELEMENTS

> Entrance Pavilions provide exhaust, heating, and air conditioning for the garage. Low LED lighting in the glass walls will guide visitors to the garage entrances at night.

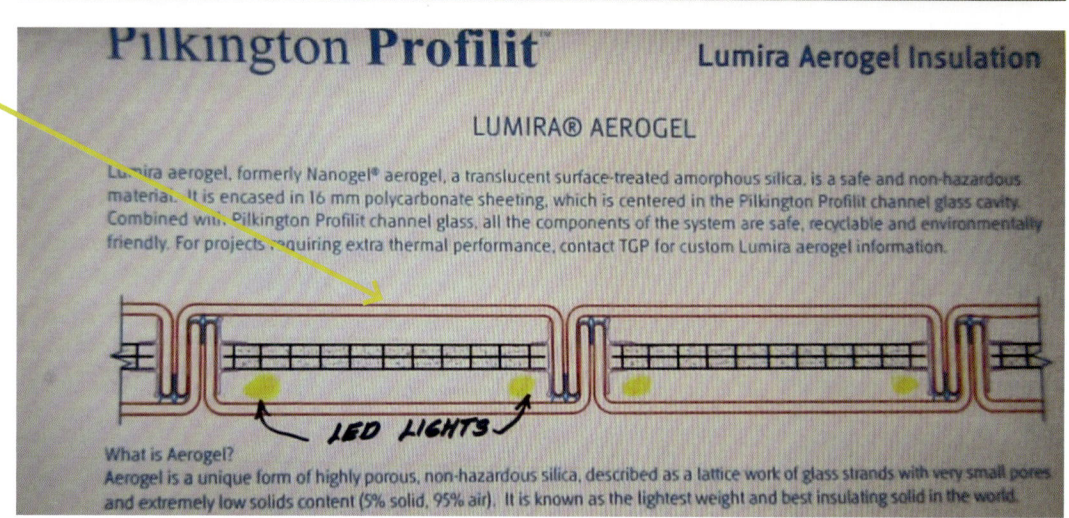

THE NATIONAL MALL UNDERGROUND

A MECHANICAL/ROBOTIC PARKING SYSTEM FOR MUSEUM VISITORS' CARS

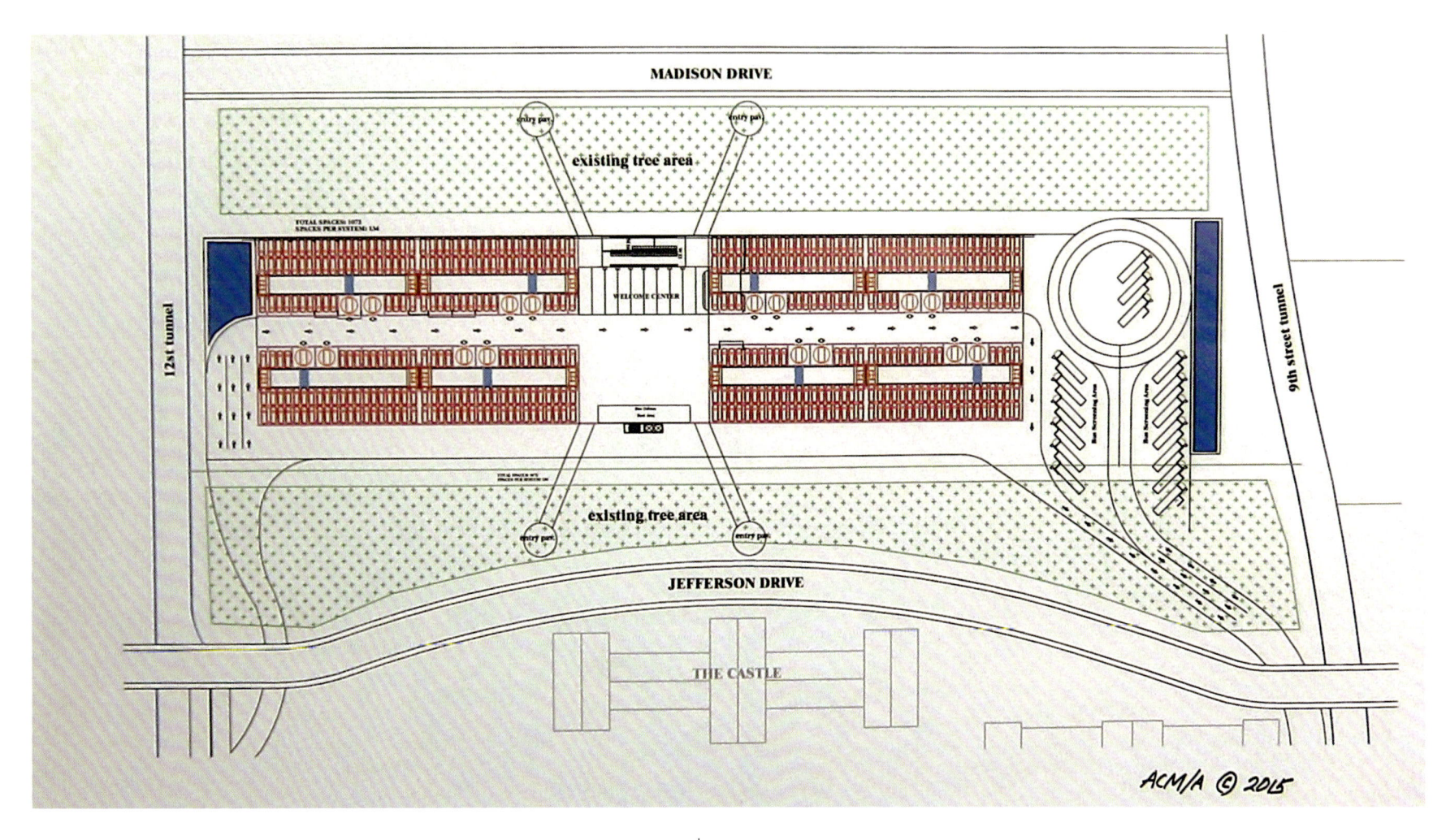

Tour buses will enter a security screening area before proceeding to the lower bus level (which is floodable) to accommodate the Constitution Avenue floods.

HOW THE ROBOTIC GARAGE WORKS

The illustration shows one car moving into the 6th garage entrance to a stop. The driver will take the car keys and go to the Visitor Center. The car will be rotated and moved by dolly onto the shuttle, which moves along the transfer aisle to a slot on the first floor—or to an elevator, which will take it to a slot on the second floor—as determined by the computer. In the number 5 exit garage, the process is reversed and the car is positioned ready to be driven away.

INSIDE THE ROBOTIC GARAGE

Inside the uninhabited mechanical/robotic garage, a dolly will move a car onto the shuttle, which will travel down the transfer aisle to reach the computer-selected garage exit. Then the dolly will move the car into that exit area, the front door will open, and the car can then be driven away.

TOUR BUS ENTRANCE TO THE ROBOTIC GARAGE

A ground cutaway view of the bus entrance, and a longer view of the mechanical/robotic parking garage.

THE NATIONAL MALL UNDERGROUND

FLOOD WATERS

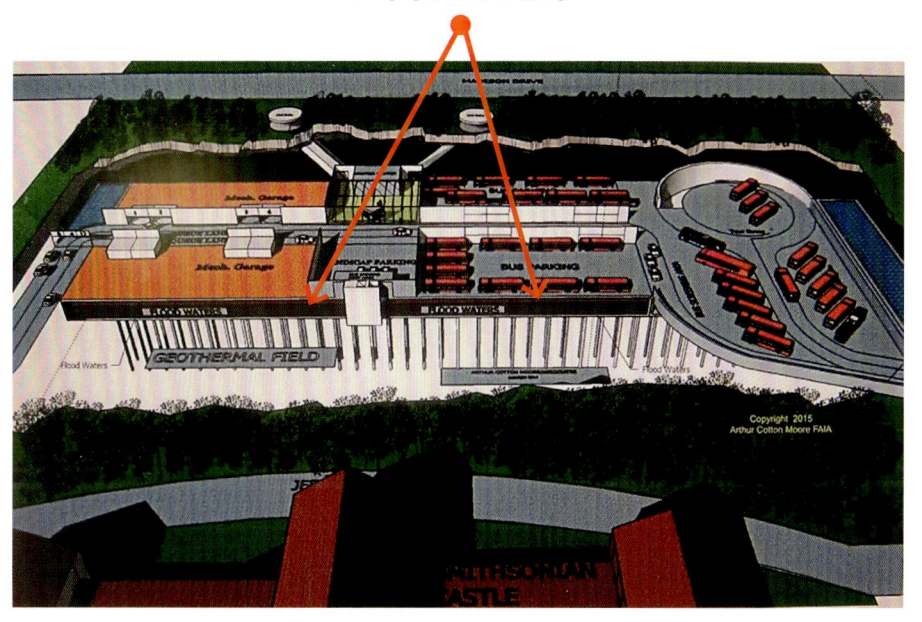

RETENTION OF STORM FLOOD WATERS FROM CONSTITUTION AVENUE

> The illustration shows the lower bus level, after buses have been removed. Some buses can be accommodated on the upper level. Portions of the mechanical/robotic garage can be designed to accommodate even more buses.

CAR ENTRANCE FROM 12th STREET RAMP

CAR ENTRANCE EXPANDED TO 3 LANES

99   Our Nation's Capital: *Pro Bono Publico* Ideas | proffered by ARTHUR COTTON MOORE FAIA ©

THE VISITOR CENTER MAIN HALL

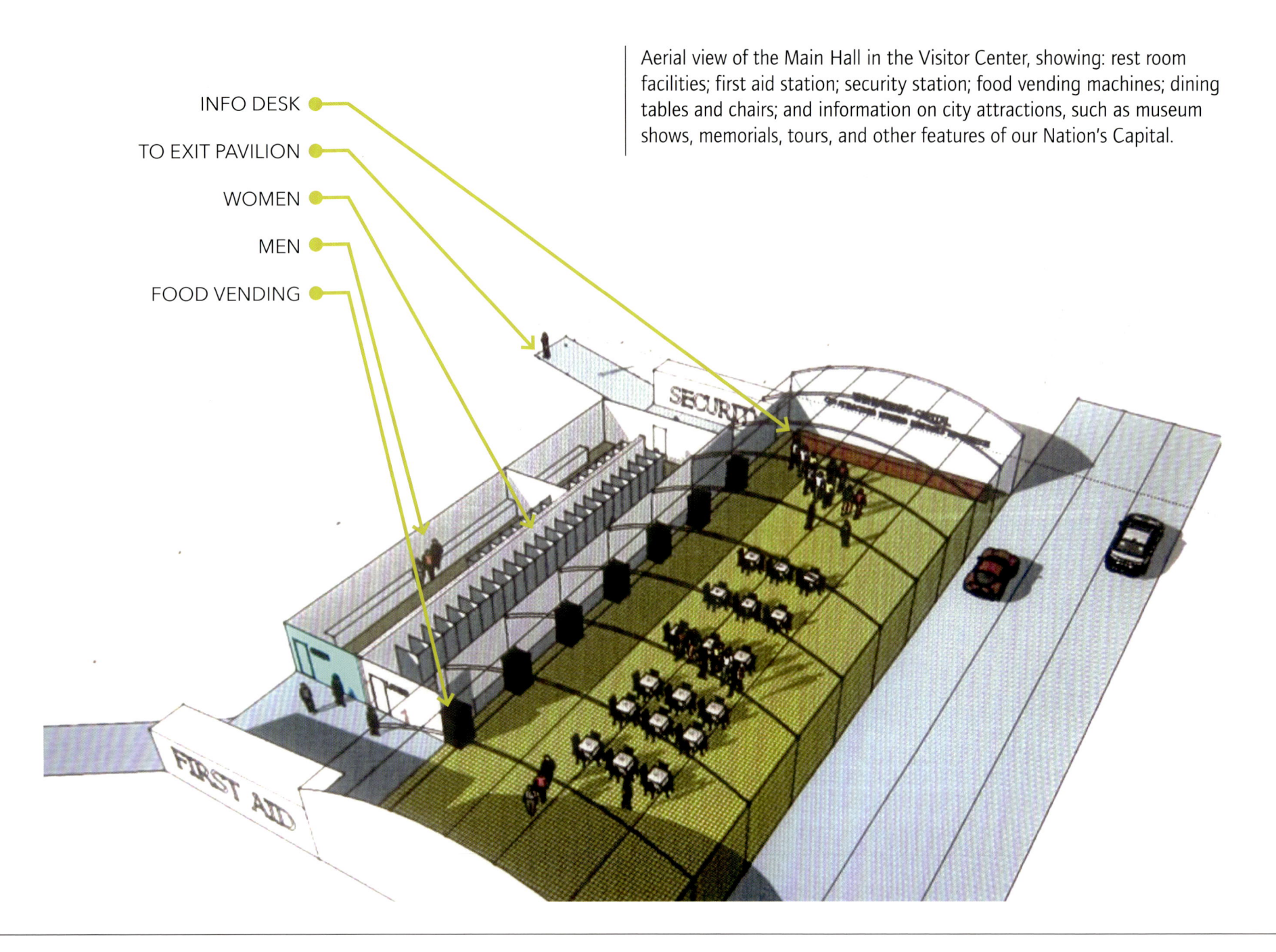

Aerial view of the Main Hall in the Visitor Center, showing: rest room facilities; first aid station; security station; food vending machines; dining tables and chairs; and information on city attractions, such as museum shows, memorials, tours, and other features of our Nation's Capital.

- INFO DESK
- TO EXIT PAVILION
- WOMEN
- MEN
- FOOD VENDING

THE NATIONAL MALL UNDERGROUND

BARREL-VAULTED MAIN HALL IN THE VISITOR CENTER

12 OUR MASTER PLAN OF THE NATIONAL MALL EXPANDED FOR THE 21st CENTURY

A Plan for a 21st Century National Mall

1. COMPLETES THE L'ENFANT AND McMILLAN PLANS
2. ESTABLISHES THE MISSING MARYLAND AVENUE
3. EXTENDS THE MALL ON THE NORTH/SOUTH AXIS
4. PROVIDES SPACE FOR NEW MEMORIALS AND MUSEUMS
5. INCREASES RECREATION FACILITIES
6. PROVIDES SECURITY FOR THE RAIL LINES
7. OPENS UP THE DEAD END OF THE WASHINGTON CHANNEL
8. COVERS UP THE INFRASTRUCTURE
9. PROVIDES A NEW VISITOR CENTER AND METRO STOP
10. RELOCATES THE SUPREME COURT TO A MORE SYMBOLIC LOCATION COMMENSURATE WITH ITS IMPORTANCE

BY ARTHUR COTTON MOORE

PENNSYLVANIA AVENUE
NEW MARYLAND AVENUE
RELOCATED SUPREME COURT BLDG.
NEW MALL EXTENSION
EXIST. GOLF COURSE

EXISTING CONFIGURATION

Our Master Plan expands the Mall to accommodate the insatiable desire for more monuments, memorials, and museums. The East/West axis of the L'Enfant and McMillan Plans cannot be expanded further, but the North/South axis can be expanded to the South.

WHITE HOUSE

PENNSYLVANIA AVENUE

CAPITOL

MARYLAND AVENUE

SUPREME COURT

NEW MEMORIAL / MUSEUMS SITES

SMALL MEMORIAL SITES

M STREET

NEW MARINAS AND RESTAURANTS

BENEFITS OF EXPANDING THE MALL

1. Completes several elements of the L'Enfant and McMillan Plans, in the form and spirit of how they were created. Our plan extends the North/South Axis of the historic plans.

2. Establishes Maryland Avenue, an unbuilt principal boulevard in the historic plans, which will provide new housing and commercial development opportunities, and also improve access to the Southwest quadrant of the city.

3. Creates much-needed new land for memorials and museums.

4. Increases the range of recreational facilities.

5. Provides improved security for rail lines serving Amtrak, Virginia Railway Express, and CSX.

6. Opens up the dead-end of the Washington Channel waterfront, giving better access up and down the river, and also provides more marinas, while retaining the golf course.

7. Bridges over and covers the existing awkward infrastructure, creating a hill-like mound, inside which would be a Metro stop on the Yellow Line.

8. Relocates the Supreme Court to a more symbolic location commensurate with its importance, to reflect the tripartite powers of our democracy.

The National Mall Coalition—founded by Judy Scott Feldman, Ph.D.—originated the need for an enlarged 3rd-Century Expansion of the Mall, and for a McMillan-type commission to bring it to reality. The Coalition presented our Master Plan at the Corcoran Gallery of Art in an effort to encourage the formation of such a commission.

SECTION THROUGH SITE PLAN FOR THE SUPREME COURT

MARYLAND AVENUE EXTENDED

Relocated Supreme Court on a structured hill spanning over the existing highways and rail line bridges.

OUR MASTER PLAN OF THE NATIONAL MALL EXPANDED FOR THE 21st CENTURY

107 Our Nation's Capital: *Pro Bono Publico* Ideas | proffered by ARTHUR COTTON MOORE FAIA ©

THE CITY OF WASHINGTON.
BIRDS-EYE VIEW FROM THE POTOMAC — LOOKING NORTH.

1880

OUR WORLD CAPITAL IN THE 21st CENTURY

In 1901, The McMillan Commission extended the boundaries of our National Mall from the Washington Monument to the Lincoln Memorial. In response to the ever-growing demand for museums and memorials within it, we follow that precedent to again stretch its boundaries—this time to the south—maintaining L'Enfant's original geometry and classical, highly symbolic, and symmetrical planning.

The eventual, inescapable extension of the Mall presents the opportunity to relocate the Supreme Court to a symbolic location south of the Jefferson Memorial, by structurally spanning over the collection of roads and rail lines to cover the awkward infrastructure. As our plan shows, that would create a symbolic green platform in the shape of a low grassy hill directly in line with the White House. That placement would achieve—for the first time in our democracy—an emblematic triangular geometry of the Executive, Legislative, and Judicial branches of our government, while further anchoring the North/South axis of the L'Enfant and McMillan Plans.

Throughout history, the culture of a nation has been the mirror of its power. When Rome was a world power, it reflected its importance in its Architecture and Art. Paris and London, each at the zenith of its dominance, also manifested its eminence on the world stage in its Art, Architecture, and Planning.

As the leading nation in the world, it is now our turn to imagine—yes, to imagine—our World Capital, not only as a symbol of our power and an exceptional example of our democracy, but also as a center for the arts, in a city of outstanding planned beauty. Such a goal requires that we Americans take the long view—over decades and generations—and keep alive our inherent American aspiration to enhance, enrich, and beautify our magnificent Nation's Capital.

ABOUT THE AUTHOR

ABOUT THE AUTHOR

Arthur Cotton Moore is a sixth-generation Washingtonian, a graduate of St. Albans School (1954), Princeton University *cum laude* (1958), and Princeton University School of Architecture (1960).

He is a national award-winning, internationally recognized architect, preservationist, planner, and painter. Since 1965, ACM has practiced in 38 cities across the United States, and has received over 70 design awards, including two National Residential Design awards from *Architectural Record* magazine, and three National AIA Honor Awards. His "Industrial Baroque" furniture series was awarded *Architectural Record* magazine's 1990 Award for Excellence in Design.

ACM projects have been published in over 2,800 articles in magazines and newspapers throughout the United States, Europe, Scandinavia, Japan, the United Kingdom, South Korea, and Australia. His projects have been included in group architectural exhibitions at the Cooper-Hewitt Museum, Columbia University's Center for the Study of American Architecture, and Columbia University's Avery Library Centennial Archive Exhibition, "Contemporary Architectural Drawings."

He has served on design award juries throughout the country, including regional and state AIA programs, as well as the country's two most prestigious: the National AIA Honor Award Program, and the National *Progressive Architecture* magazine Design Award Jury. He is one of 600 architects around the world included since 1980 in all editions of the British compilation *Contemporary Architects*, published by St. James Press, which recognizes architects on an international level. He is included in Wikipedia's "The List of Notable Architects—well-known individuals with a large body of published work/notable structures."

ACM has traveled to 132 countries, many of them multiple times, to photograph and study their architecture, and has written on architecture, urban affairs, preservation, and art.

He has lectured widely at universities and professional conferences, including several lectures at the Smithsonian Institution, where in 1978 he gave a four-part series entitled "The Architecture of the Absurd." In 1979 he gave the Annual Guest Lecture at Trinity College in Dublin. In 1982 he gave the Henry Hornbostel Memorial Lecture at Carnegie-Mellon University, and in 1985 was invited by the Hirshhorn Museum to give a retrospective lecture on his work, marking the 20th anniversary of his practice.

Since 1990, ACM has had solo painting exhibitions in New York, Chicago, Washington, and Paris, and has participated in group painting shows in New York and Cologne. His 1995 traveling museum exhibition, *Visions of the Future*, was shown in museums in the Czech Republic and Poland. His first book, *The Powers of Preservation*, which focused on his historic building work and urban planning projects, was published by McGraw-Hill in 1998. His novel, *Interruption of the Cocktail Hour: A Washington Yarn of Art, Murder, and the Attempted Assassination of the President,* was published in 2014. *Washington Comics*, a book of irreverent paintings depicting the absurdities of our Nation's Capital, will be published in 2018.

He lives in Washington, D.C., with his wife, Patricia Moore.